Endorsements

My friend Geoff Peters is a uniquely authentic leader who has the gift of engaging anyone, anywhere, through the power of story. In this book, Geoff combines candor, humor, and a refreshing use of Scripture to weave together the power of his personal story with the story of God. As I read it, I was drawn to how God uses our experiences, no matter how challenging, for his purposes and his mission. I encourage you to pick up this book and find how you too can say yes to playing your role in God's love story.

—**Jeff Holck, DMiss**
Director of Partnerships and Training,
Fuller Center for Spiritual Formation
Adjunct Assistant Professor of Leadership,
Fuller Theological Seminary

Love Child reminds us of God's grand Love story, and how he has written humanity (that's us) into that story as his representatives to live out his love on earth. Geoff uses both his own story, told very vulnerably, and recent research that he commissioned globally to show the massive gap in our understanding of what representing God looks like, and who can and should do it. Like Geoff, I honor the past, but with him I am convinced that much has to change in our structures, our programs, our language, and what we believe about ourselves if we are to see followers of Jesus fully embrace their created purpose. *Love Child* will help you reflect on these things and hopefully give you courage and the heart of love needed to make seismic shifts in your life and the world around you. This book is not for those who are content with where they are and believe we are living up to our potential as the body of Christ. It's for those who believe otherwise and want some guidance for a new direction.

—**Andrew Scott**
Past President and CEO, Operation Mobilization (USA)
Cofounder, Scatter Global
Author, *Scatter: Go Therefore and Take Your Job with You*

We're in a place of huge disruption as a society and as churches. The leadership systems and training we have in place as God's people are failing us. Any engagement with this unraveling requires a transformed understanding of who we are before God. This is what Geoff is chronicling for us. More than a personal journey filled with critical and helpful stories, Geoff points us toward the "one thing that matters" for the renewal of leadership in this strange new place.

—ALAN J. ROXBURGH
The Missional Network

In *Love Child* Geoff Peters invites us to live more deeply in the adventure of Christian believing and living. I use those three words on purpose: Peters is serious about shaping faith in the God who loves us, but he is no less committed to displaying the God who sends us to live and serve in the world. He does this through a collection of honest and vulnerable reflections on God's work through his own experiences in childhood and marriage, parenthood and work, mission and ministry, in both successes and failures. In the end, the reader finds that *Love Child* is both a description and a command—a reminder of who we are (loved by God) and who we are called to be: children of a God who sends us to love. For Christians seeking to renew their sense of identity and calling, or for those who may be meeting Jesus for the first time, Peters offers a wonderful gift in *Love Child*.

—REV. JEFFREY CONKLIN-MILLER, ThD
Learning Lead and Tutor in Evangelism and Missiology,
Cliff College, Derbyshire, UK

I resonate with Geoff's belief that God is more interested in our willingness to follow his commands than he is in the result of our work. Having worked closely with women who are ministering cross-culturally for the past twenty-two years, I hear the struggle of wanting to see the fruit of our investment in the lives of those who do not yet know Christ. *We want to measure the kingdom impact we are having and have a success story to tell our sending churches and supporters!* What is the Lord asking you to do to participate in God's work in the world? I believe reading this book will help bring clarity and inspiration to the Lord's invitation to you. Listen well!

—**Lorrie Lindgren**
CEO, Thrive Ministry

LOVE CHILD

A Journey through Scandal to Sacred Mission

GEOFF PETERS

visit us at missionbooks.org

Love Child: A Journey through Scandal to Sacred Mission

© 2025 by Geoff Peters. All rights reserved.
Previously published as *Made to Love* © 2022 by Geoff Peters.

No part of this book may be reproduced, stored in a retrieval system, or transmitted in any form or by any means—electronic, mechanical, photocopy, recording, or otherwise—without prior written permission from the publisher, except brief quotations used in connection with reviews in magazines or newspapers.
For permission, email: permissions@wclbooks.com.
For corrections, email editor@wclbooks.com.

All Scripture quotations, unless otherwise indicated, are taken from the Holy Bible, New International Version®, NIV®. Copyright ©1973, 1978, 1984, 2011 by Biblica, Inc.™ Used by permission of Zondervan. All rights reserved worldwide. www.zondervan.com. The "NIV" and "New International Version" are trademarks registered in the United States Patent and Trademark Office by Biblica, Inc.™

Scripture quotations marked "ESV" are taken from The ESV® Bible (The Holy Bible, English Standard Version®), copyright © 2001 by Crossway, a publishing ministry of Good News Publishers. Used by permission. All rights reserved.

Published by William Carey Publishing
10 W. Dry Creek Cir
Littleton, CO 80120 | www.missionbooks.org

William Carey Publishing is a ministry of Frontier Ventures
Pasadena, CA 91114 | www.frontierventures.org

Cover and Interior Design: Mike Riester

ISBNs: 978-1-64508-638-3 (paperback)
       978-1-64508-640-6 (epub)

Printed Worldwide

29 28 27 26 25   1 2 3 4 5   IN

Library of Congress Control Number: 2024950353

Para Belén, mi amor.

Definition: **love child** (noun)

1: a child whose parents were not married when the child was conceived; the child of an affair

2: something (such as a project or collaboration) that is a product of hard work and devotion

Contents

1	The Devil of a Time	1
2	The Best Kept Secret. Ever.	13
3	Please Accept My Apology	25
4	The Phantom and the Opera	31
5	Naked and Afraid	37
6	Checkmate	45
7	Let's Talk	55
8	Getting Served by Miss Addie	61
9	Take It Out of the Box	65
10	The Tools of the Trade	71
11	The Original Marketer	81
12	How Then Shall We Live?	89
13	Fruitless	95
14	Chris-Cross	101
15	White-Knuckle Grip	107
16	Chocolate or Vanilla	119
17	Free to Love	127
18	Going Septic	139
19	Get Up and Go	149
20	Oh My Soul, Korea	157
21	The Greatest Love Story of All Time	167
22	A Father's Love	173
Afterword		183
Acknowledgments		185
Notes		186
About the Author		187

1

The Devil of a Time

There is no normal life that is free of pain. It's the very wrestling with our problems that can be the impetus for our growth.
—Mister Rogers

I am the bastard son of a priest and a nun.

We can't help the circumstances we're born into, but that doesn't mean they don't color the starting line for our life. My start was a scandal. My start was wrapped in shock, anger, disbelief, disappointment and sadness.

Two families ashamed. A church outraged. Welcome to the world.

To be completely accurate, my mother was not a nun at the time I was conceived. She was a petite, twenty-six-year-old brunette from the heart of Arizona, who had hazel eyes and a shattered spirit. When I think about her at that time in 1976, I envision a scared and bewildered girl lacking any sort of direction—like a golden finch that had been hurt and caged by its master, until one day it discovered a hole in the wirework.

My mom had been married to a man who abused her physically. He was the kind of guy who would take the dog for a run by pulling him along on dirt roads behind his truck, returning home with the dog so exhausted he could barely make it back inside, his raw paws leaving bloody footprints on the cracked cement.

LOVE CHILD

From what I understand, my mom suffered a lot at the hands of men and boys throughout her upbringing, so it doesn't surprise me that she chose an abusive man to be her husband. When we are broken, our judgment is often broken too. Or sometimes we simply run to what's familiar. We do what we know, even when it hurts us.

Finally summoning the courage to leave her husband, my mother sought the counsel of the church—and specifically of the man who would become my father, an Episcopal priest.

As life would have it, he too was broken. My father was married but starved for love and care. He and his wife met in seminary, and they had two children with special needs. They struggled to take care of them, living and operating in survival mode, in their own little self-contained boxes. She became bitter and detached; he became sad and lonely. To my father, their marriage was cold and loveless. There was no warmth. No care. No emotional connection.

I know counseling is an intimate situation. It requires talking about deeply personal experiences, feelings, memories, and fears. That's why I can only imagine the risk of these two broken people meeting together in a room: one with a pastoral nature and a hollow marriage, yet a genuine desire to bring hope and healing to a suffering woman; and the hurting woman, revealing her painful past and darkest days with this man who seemed to care for her deeply—not hurting her, as others before him.

Sigmund Freud once said that within the context of psychotherapy, "It will never be possible to avoid little laboratory explosions." In hindsight, you don't have to be clairvoyant to anticipate the potential for chemistry between my parents. Yet that doesn't make the result any more palatable to people. The product of their relationship was scandalous to the church and horrifying to my mother's family.

I was painful for each of my parents in different ways.

When my father learned of my mom's pregnancy, he grieved. His unfaithfulness to his wife and to God was not a problem that could be ignored. There would soon be a child … a living, breathing bundle of proof of his marital infidelity. Of sacred lines that had been crossed. Of the kind of sin that causes great shame and heavy repercussions, both at home and—when the church is your boss—at work.

With a heavy heart, my father made an appointment with the bishop and confessed. The bishop instructed him to step up and be a strong provider for the baby. He had sinned, and now he needed to do the right thing.

When my mother shared the news with her family, she received a mixed reception. Some thought she should have an abortion. Others wanted her to give me up for adoption. One person, my grandfather, pushed for her to keep me. I think the others were reacting out of a sense of shame and of fear for my mother's future. She already had a failed marriage on the record of her young life. And now she was going to give birth to a baby conceived with a married priest? What would people think? I would imagine that my mom's fate as the black sheep of her family was thereby forever sealed.

I was born at St. Joseph's Hospital in Tucson, Arizona, in 1977. Six weeks later, my father met me for the first time. My mom invited him to a drive-up motel near the Tucson airport, where she allowed him to hold me and then announced that she was leaving—for good. My father now tells me how this pained him, how he wanted to have a relationship with me but realized in that motel room that it wasn't going to happen. My mother wanted to get away and start over. No doubt at the urging of family, she needed to put yet another traumatic chapter behind her, this time with an illegitimate child in tow.

I'm told there were letters and photos from my father for a few years, until they stopped. It actually was decades before I had an enjoyable meeting with him. It was at that time, as an adult, that I found out my father had prayed for me by name each day throughout my childhood.

As an adult who has traveled a long, twisty road with God, when I think of that—of my father talking with God about me, asking for his protection and blessing upon me—it allows me to think generously of him. And yet I know that as a child, I wasn't benevolent. I didn't want prayers. I didn't want good intentions. I wanted a dad.

After the meeting in the hotel room, my mom and I began our journey together. You'd think she would have run away from the church, but she didn't. She stayed.

My mom raised me in a deeply religious environment. We went to church multiple times each week, sometimes multiple times a day. I was in church choirs from a very young age, and I also served as an acolyte, or altar boy. With my mom, faith was assumed. It's what we did. There was no other option.

My mom was a strong faith role model, but our life was chaotic and unpredictable. Or perhaps it's more accurate to say that our life was chaotic and unpredictable, yet my mom still managed to be a great faith role model. I suppose it's true both ways.

Actually, to say our life was "unstable" doesn't really do it justice. We were always on food stamps and other forms of government assistance. We didn't live on the streets, thanks to the help of friends and family, but we were often pretty darn close to being homeless. I remember living back in Tucson when I was ten. On summer days when the temperature soared over 100 degrees, I'd run across the scalding hot street barefoot with a food stamp clutched in my hand and the goal of buying a three-cent piece of Bazooka Joe bubble gum—the ones with the comics—so that my mom and I could get the change to do some laundry. We eventually got a washer from someone, but drying clothes was always a mix of putting them on the line or laying them over the oven door with the heat on low. I lost more than a few pairs of jeans to browning because we'd left them on the oven door too long.

For most kids, school is one of the constants in their lives. But I changed schools every single year—sometimes twice, and one year three times. All in all, I changed schools thirteen times before my sophomore year of high school. Sometimes it was because we moved and sometimes it was because I had been kicked out of the school, the district, or at one point, the state of Arizona.

I was a nightmare for my teachers.

I started fights, misbehaved, and had uncontrollable outbursts. While I was in second grade, my mother had me admitted twice to a local inpatient psychiatric facility—once after I threw a knife at her and the other time after I gave a classmate a concussion during a playground game. Inside the facility, they'd draw my blood daily and monitor my brainwaves to help me learn to relax. They tried to teach us a lot of skills and mechanisms to manage our behavior and life, but it all felt cold and impersonal. The furniture was stiff and sterile, the walls were glass, and overall it was a very uncomfortable place to try to get comfortable while they "healed" our young brains.

LOVE CHILD

To pass the time, we used to send messages back and forth by writing notes on tiny pieces of paper, stuffing them into the center holes of the wooden erector set wheels, and rolling them across the hall while the staff had their backs turned. I don't think we had anything important to say to each other. We certainly weren't plotting to overthrow the place. We just needed to remember that despite our horrible circumstances, we were still kids.

I don't blame my mom for sending me away. As a single parent, I can't imagine the stress of having a child like me. I was reacting out of my broken and unstable reality. I was too young to be reasoned with but big enough to physically traumatize everyone within my wingspan. I have no doubt my mom prayed for my cure. I would guess that at the same time, my absence felt like an opportunity for her to put on her own oxygen mask for a while.

For me, the psychiatric facility was a scary place. It took me away from my mom, who was the only remotely constant human in my life. I was in the care of strangers in white coats who were trying to "fix" me because I was so broken and unlikeable that only paid professionals, rather than family, could take on the job. As a child in a psychiatric facility in the 80s, my pockets were emptied of the currency of trust. I filled the space with self-reliance, holding onto my defiant belief that independence was the only thing I could depend on.

After my second stay in the facility, my antics continued, and I was given an IQ test because my teachers couldn't understand how I could complete all of my work properly but still behave so horribly in class. After that they shipped me off to a gifted and talented school within the district. But by the end of the school year I had been suspended multiple times and the school district requested that I not come back for third grade.

As my behavior continued to escalate, and my paper trail grew, the state of Arizona instructed my mother to choose from two options:
1. Send Geoff to a foster family inside the state, or
2. Send Geoff to live with family outside the state

Both options were basically a one-year time-out away from my mother, so my mom opted for the second and shipped me off to my uncle in Northern California for fourth grade.

My uncle was a large man, probably 6'4" and 250 pounds or more. I quickly learned that my "different state, same state of mind" plan wasn't going to work with him. The first time I acted up, he grabbed the back of my belt and lifted me off the floor with one hand, carrying me into my room and throwing me on the bed to cool off. The rest of that year went much more smoothly.

In the following years I racked up more suspensions as I bounced between California and Arizona. Then my behavior, language, and general lack of respect crossed the line enough that my mother sent me away again, this time for ninth grade, to a group home run by the Roman Catholic Church.

Hanna Boys Center is a group home facility located in a beautiful part of Sonoma, California—not that I really appreciated the surroundings. Half of the boys at the home were there at the request of their parents and the others were directed there by the state. It wasn't technically a juvenile detention facility, but they screened all our mail. And if we attempted to leave the campus without permission, officers with dogs from the sheriff's department were deployed to find us.

For the next fifteen months, my roommates and schoolmates were a wild mix of trouble and fun from all over California. There were boys from "good homes" and boys from Oakland gangs. Some were quiet and putting in their time, others were determined to burn the place down—literally. One night the boy three doors down from me, Mike, pulled Jesus from the crucifix on the wall and broke him into pieces. I was hit in the face with one of Jesus' legs as Mike yelled, "The Body of Christ!"

We were all a pretty disturbed bunch. It was here that I learned to make a slim jim, a tool for unlocking car doors, and was eventually arrested for attempting to steal a car.

To pay the bill for this brief incarceration, the boarding school wanted my mom to reach out to my father for financial assistance. They were a "pay what you can" facility, and what my mom could pay was clearly not enough to meet the lowest bar. After a letter, a judge, and some lawyers, my father started to pay a bit of child support from that point forward.

After finishing the year at the boarding school, my mom promised to let me come home and stay at one school for the remainder of my high school years. This gave me a sense of security I hadn't experienced before.

When I started high school, I immediately auditioned for the top choir on campus and made it. All my years singing at church had paid off! Choir and band quickly became my touchstones in high school, and as such, the majority of my friends were music nerds. Even though they were a tight group that had been friends for years, they welcomed me. To fit in with them, I behaved well during the school day.

The nights and weekends were a different story. I hung out with a darker crowd. Instead of singing *The*

Lord Bless You and Keep You or *Danny Boy*, my Saturday nights were filled with drinking, graffiti, vandalism, arson, and shooting up local businesses with handguns. We would even hood-surf on my friend Matt's '67 Mustang while he drove 80 miles per hour down an unlit dusty dirt road with his lights off. Then Monday would come around and I'd be back on the choir risers.

I was one boy living two very different lives.

I know I was an angry kid. I had a lot to be angry about. I had been abandoned by my father. I had a very unstable existence with no constancy of school, care, or friends. I had no lasting relationships. And I was sent away every other year to a family member or facility, for anywhere from a couple of weeks to over a year each time. I never knew what was coming at me. My only "normal" was that I had myself to rely upon—no one else.

I remember being very afraid that people at my high school would figure out just how poor my mom and I were. I had a white Adidas sweatshirt that I loved to wear because it said "tennis camp" on it. For me, it represented the kind of sweatshirt you'd wear if your family had a decent income and a dog. So I was horrified when one of my classmates asked me which tennis camp I had attended because he had also attended that camp. I lied and said I was borrowing the sweatshirt from a friend.

I felt ashamed of my poverty. It was a daily fear that I would be exposed for all that I didn't have. It was safer to keep people at a distance.

Considering all the time I spent at church, some people who know my story are amazed that I didn't get angry at God. They wonder why it never occurred to me to blame him for the injustices of my life—or to plead my case for a better life. For a boy so rife with rage, so wounded by his circumstances, how was I able to sing hymns at church each week, repeat the liturgy, and never make the connection that God cared about me on a personal level? And while I was out carousing with my weekend friends, why didn't I tag the church, set fire to the chapel, or smash up the stained-glass windows?

It's a fair question. When I was a kid, God was an idea and the church was an unquestionable mainstay of my life. The church was a constant—a home—and you don't graffiti your home. Wherever we lived, we always found the church. In every community, it was there. It was probably the only consistently familiar element of my young life.

"The Lord be with you."

"And also with you."

The rhythm of the Eucharist prayer, the hymns, the order of service, the colors on the altar … these were the universal threads that connected the Episcopal and Anglican parishes wherever we were. Even when I was the new kid at church, I knew what to say and do. I could fit in. I felt a sense of stability in knowing what the worship service was going to be like.

Yet while the church felt comfortable to me, there was nothing relational or personal about it. God felt distant to me—and wholly uninterested in my life or circumstances. Similarly, my mother was always sending me away, and my father (who was God's representative on earth as a priest) was so indifferent that he left when I was six weeks old.

I remember one of the counselors at my ninth-grade group home declaring that because I was "the bastard son of a fallen priest," I was number one on the devil's list—as if to say that God had no use for me, but the devil did have plans for me.

The Devil of a Time

My chaotic, frenzied, and disjointed childhood added depth and color to the redemption story of my life. Yes, I have been uniquely remade; and yes, my past experiences still shape who I am.

That's the beauty of the body of Christ. It's comprised of many people—none of us perfect—all following the direction of the One who remade our lives in the first place.

For all of us, our past is a part of our story. And God will use it for his mission.

2

The Best Kept Secret. Ever.

> *There is no conversion that does not produce the seed of a loving life, tiny though it be in the beginning.*
> —**George Verwer**, *The Revolution of Love*

I remember seeing a YouTube video years ago that was one of those word-association exercises. The YouTuber would say a word like *purple* or *chocolate*, and the random person on the street who was being interviewed would say the first words that entered his or her mind. Faith-based words were also included in the mix. When the YouTuber said *Christian*, folks responded with words like "judgmental" and "two-faced." When he said *Jesus*, people responded with words like "loving" and "defender" and "stood up for the poor."

How can this be? How can the perception of Christians—Jesus' representatives here on earth—be in complete opposition to the very nature of Jesus? If we extrapolate the insights gleaned from this one little YouTube-documented experiment, is it any wonder that people are no longer attracted to the church, which is made up of Christians?

Why can't the public see Jesus in our churches? I think the answer is rooted in two issues. I'll call them the formula and the secret. They may just be the secret formula we need to change the current trajectory and start bringing people back to faith in Christ.

The Formula
What the church has been telling us about faith

I believe the Christian church of modern times is fixated on numbers.

The following questions can be heard regularly at almost any church leadership meeting across America. "How many visitors did we have last weekend?" "What's our goal for next year's capital campaign?" "How many conversions did we document at our Easter service?" "How many souls did we win for Christ last year?" "If we make the service time thirty minutes later, do you think we'll lose the regulars who like to go to brunch after the service, or will we gain more young adults who want to sleep in longer?" "Should we take away some of the chairs next week to make the sanctuary feel fuller?" (OK, in fairness, I myself asked this one when I was a pastor.)

Now let me be clear: I love data. It has the power to reveal trends, identify potential problems and opportunities, and shed light on gaps. Without question, data is a virtual gold mine of possibilities. I'd even go so far as to say that data represents one of the ways we can see where the Holy Spirit is moving. Within the context of the church, however, I think we've allowed data to give us the false sense that we hold the keys to kingdom growth—that we can somehow strategize our way to drawing people in.

I believe that many church-leadership teams have waded too far into the "run your church like a business" end of the pool. They'll tell you that to be healthy they need to understand and track their metrics to ensure they are growing in a steady, fiscally responsible manner. Yet there's a deceivingly fine line between exercising good stewardship and asserting imagined control.

As humans, we like control. We want to know that if we eat five hundred fewer calories each day, then we will lose one or two pounds each week. If we cut our expenses each month by $150, then we can pay off our car loan in seven months.

If-then statements like this start with a hypothesis and are followed by a conclusion. You might remember them from a math class. You also might recognize them from your Sunday worship services:

- If you repeat this very specific prayer, then you are a Christ follower.
- If you make these three practices a part of your daily journey, then you will grow in your Christian maturity.
- If you become a member of this church, then you will be on the path toward spiritual transformation.

This desire to control our outcomes is a very human trait; and the church, which is run by humans, often reflects this instinct.

I know it's completely normal for us to try to achieve a desired effect through our own doing. For those of us who work as leaders, it's more common than not for us not to just think, but to really and truly believe that our unique brand of button-pushing and lever-pulling is what causes success.

Yet God doesn't work that way. The results of our evangelistic efforts are not up to us. No priest or pastor directs God's process of calling souls to himself. There's nothing linear about faith. It's not a ladder to climb. There isn't a methodical, three-step program or golden pathway.

The mysterious work and movement of the Holy Spirit in our hearts is like water or air. It can't be plotted on a graph, and it can't be contained. Despite our best efforts, it can't be fully understood by human minds.

Initiative and planning are important, but I think the organized church has often doubled down on thinking and strategizing when we should be focused on prayer and action.

The ultimate joy for every pastor I know is when he or she sees a life transformed. When someone gets it—really gets it. When faith in Christ clicks and sticks. But we can't measure that. It's the work of the Holy Spirit, and as Christians who are leading others to Christ, we just point the way.

Is it even possible for us humans to measure what a transformed life looks like? We often love to judge the transformation of others in comparison to ourselves, but why do we feel the need to do that? And what does the endgame even look like anyway? The only example in Scripture is a life that fully exhibits the fruit of the Spirit.

> The fruit of the Spirit is love, joy, peace, forbearance, kindness, goodness, faithfulness, gentleness and self-control. (Gal 5:22–23)

Just to be clear, it is *fruit*, not *fruits*. It's one fruit, with many traits. For example, an apple is sweet, red, crunchy, and off-white under the skin.

Whenever one of these traits is not present, it should be a red flag for us that something is wrong. If you bite into an apple and the flesh is brown, or it isn't crunchy, or there is no sweetness, you know something isn't right. The fruit of the Spirit is our own personal litmus test.

The Best Kept Secret. Ever.

It's our own way of self-identifying our closeness with God. If one of these traits is missing in my life at any point in time, then I clearly have some spiritual transforming to do.

In his book *The Four Loves*, C. S. Lewis says, "A man's spiritual health is exactly proportional to his love for God." In other words, if I'm not feeling joy in my life, I'm probably not close enough to the Source of true joy!

Nonetheless, church leaders have had a strong drive to measure corporate transformation based on outward professions of faith, because a self-reported profession would supposedly indicate that a person is going to live a good Christian life. But data on this shows that professions of faith don't always correlate with a life lived for Christ.

A fascinating study explored the psychology of conversion and the ability of religious and spiritual transformation to foster positive change in people's lives.[4] The study collected data from adolescents attending Christian summer camp. The youth were evaluated before the camp, immediately after the camp, and many months later. Here's the kicker: there was no correlation between those who made a first-time commitment or a recommitment of faith and those who were living a more Christ-centered life many months later.

A faith decision is a moment in time, but being a disciple is a lifelong journey. The decision alone is important, of course, but it's just the beginning.

True spiritual transformation isn't the result of a formula, a single prayer, or a three-step process. It is something we can prayerfully, humbly, earnestly choose to pursue every day. We don't need to cover our bases by jumping through hoops. We need to surrender fully to God with our whole hearts and lives. Jesus taught us to pray "thy will be done" and "give us today our daily bread." It's as simple as that. The Lord is inviting us to trust him and be available for him and his purposes. That's all.

The Secret
What the church hasn't been telling us about faith

Imagine you are going for a walk in your neighborhood one day and you approach the local park. Amid the swing sets and sandboxes and park benches and ducks are throngs of people. People of all ages. People who are smiling and talking and hugging. People who laugh out loud, people who are deep in conversation, people who have their arms around others who are tearful.

"I wonder what's going on here?" you ask yourself. Just then, a woman walks toward you. "Hi! What is this?" you ask.

"It's our weekly neighborhood block party!" she says. "We love to gather as neighbors, do life together, and serve each other and the community. Come and join us!"

It seems harmless, so you walk alongside her. She introduces you to people, all the while asking questions about you. She wants to know about your family, where you come from, and what kind of hobbies you enjoy. The thing that strikes you most about this woman is that she really wants to hear your answers. She isn't just asking to be polite. You can tell she truly cares.

"Yes! This is exactly what my life has been missing!" you say to your new friend. "I'm in! When do we get together next? Why don't more people know about this?"

"Oh, we spread the word all the time!" the woman responds. "We have a team of specialists, like me, who reach out to our community and promote our gatherings. If you'd like to join the outreach committee, we meet once a month. I think we may have an opening."

For generations, this has been the experience of the majority of churchgoers in America. On one hand, we want everyone to invite their neighbors. On the other hand, we form special committees, or designate certain people with labels which communicate that outreach and discipleship is their responsibility. We say it's for everyone. Our systems and structures say otherwise.

But outreach and discipleship were *never* meant to be the work of a few. John 20 makes this crystal clear and is, I believe, one of the most remarkable passages of the Bible. It's the end of the Easter narrative and the evening of resurrection day. Jesus has risen from the grave, but the disciples are scared of being found and treated to the same fate. They are gathered together in a locked room, when Christ appears.

> On the evening of that first day of the week, when the disciples were together, with the doors locked for fear of the Jewish leaders, Jesus came and stood among them and said, "Peace be with you!" After he said this, he showed them his hands and side. The disciples were overjoyed when they saw the Lord.
>
> Again Jesus said, "Peace be with you! As the Father has sent me, I am sending you." (John 20:19–21)

Did you catch that last part? **I am sending you.**

Does it sound like Jesus wanted to relegate sharing his message of love and hope to a short-term program or designate it as an activity for specialists only? Do you think Jesus would have asked his disciples to review a pamphlet with people, highlighting the top three reasons he is the answer, along with a pre-written prayer? Would he have wanted us to track conversions and make it less about people and more about building our own conversion portfolios?

I don't think so either. Yet that's the approach the church has so often taken. By treating God's mission as the work of a ministry team, and funding it as such, we Christians have been able to pass the buck, quite literally. "We give to our church's missions team," is synonymous with "Great Commission? Check!"

But "missions" was never designed to be something the church **does**. It is supposed to be what the church body **is**.

> Therefore go and make disciples of all nations, baptizing them in the name of the Father and of the Son and of the Holy Spirit, and teaching them to obey everything I have commanded you. And surely I am with you always, to the very end of the age. (Matt 28:19–20)

The church's purpose—our purpose—is to advance God's mission. And Paul tells us this calling is for everyone, not just the missionaries. In fact, the word *missionary* isn't even in the Bible! It's just a word we've used over the years to designate people who leave home or go overseas for the sake of the gospel.

> We are therefore Christ's ambassadors, as though God were making his appeal through us. (2 Cor 5:20)

We are called to love others. *All of us!* And when we serve others, we are serving God. This is not something that was meant to be relinquished to full-time professionals, a committee, or a subset of the church body.

One of my professors in seminary—a lifelong missionary himself—once commented that perhaps the invention of full-time clergy and full-time missionaries was the biggest barrier to the spread of the gospel in church history. That's a bold statement! But his point was simple: when we made full-time ministry a profession, we made it a career. And once it was a career, it made everyone with dreams of becoming bakers and doctors and teachers and hairdressers and accountants feel like they had to make a choice: give up their passions or "work" in the church. As a result, it made it a whole lot easier to leave the missionary work to a special select few.

So here's the big secret: if you are a Christian, *you are a missionary*. There is really no difference between the two.

Sharing the love of Christ is your calling. It's what you signed up for when you chose to follow Christ. And guess what? There's no one way to do it. You were uniquely made to reach others for him using your own traits, quirks, and style.

We can skip the confusing, triangulated relationship the church has created between each of us and Jesus. On the one hand, we're taught to build a personal, one-on-one relationship with him. On the other hand, we're led to believe that he must like healthy church-membership rosters, triumphant salvation stories, and strong conversion numbers. That sounds like a Jesus who is more interested in the business of the church than in the hearts of his followers. I don't believe this was the church's intent, but I do believe we have missed the point.

It's time for Christ followers to follow Christ. This is the "so what" in the Easter story. We weren't redeemed just so we could live a better life. We've been sent out! We've been called!

Pastor and best-selling author of books like *Crazy Love*, Francis Chan, relates it this way,

> We're all called to be disciple makers to some degree. You may not reach hundreds, but you can reach a few! … Some people are discontent in their lives and they think it's because of their career or life situation. But it's because you were made to be his witnesses. There is so much peace when you're actually doing your job. This is where we come alive!

LOVE CHILD

As Pastor Mark Batterson says, Jesus did not die to keep us safe and have us do easy things. Yet a lot of churches create environments and programs that do just that—feed people in safe, protected "cages." There's a cage for youth group, a cage for college students, a cage for adults, and a host of other cages for specialty groups. We all sit in our cages and wait to be fed, knowing all the while that we don't belong there. Yet it's safe, and kind of nice to be taken care of, so we make ourselves comfortable.

It's pretty clear: the church has domesticated Christ's followers. Instead of focusing on releasing people into the world, church leaders have focused on keeping people safe under the protective awning of the church. But cages and hand-feeding ultimately steal our true, God-given spirit. We need to return to our native surroundings and embrace the lives we were created to pursue. We need to live out our faith in our neighborhoods and workplaces and greater communities, trading the convenience of the cage for the excitement of living as God intended. Our mission is to show people who don't know Jesus what his love really looks like through our natural, normal, uncaged lives. We can do that! All it takes is a willingness to embrace an unpredictable adventure and live life in the wild.

Make no mistake, God loves you. He has saved you and redeemed you for his purpose. Remember all that talk about giving him your life? Remember the talk about dying to yourself and being born again? It's all for his mission, his goals for humanity and the world.

It doesn't matter if you came from a family of Christians, of another faith background, or of no faith at all. It doesn't matter if you lived as a good person right up to the time you chose to follow Christ, or if you lived as an outcast and a rebel. When you said yes, you opted in.

The Best Kept Secret. Ever.

You joined a movement of Jesus followers who can trace our calling and purpose back to that little locked room where the first disciples were huddled together, when Jesus showed up with a simple message: "I am sending you."

You have already been called. You have been called to love a broken world and to help make sure that everyone on the planet knows what Christ's real and genuine love is about.

I came to this understanding later in life. I was raised in the church, but somehow this part of the story didn't click until later. But now I know why God redeemed me.

Contrary to my ninth-grade counselor's prediction of an apprenticeship with the devil, I am a man with a deep-seated passion to see people come alive as they discover, pursue, and invest in God's work. Nothing brings me greater joy than watching people make genuine, loving connections with others for God's glory.

Of course, we are all a work in progress. I most certainly am. That's why I feel so compelled to address topics in this book that are potentially uncomfortable for the church. It's not to point fingers, cast blame, or declare who's doing it right and who's doing it wrong. It's about reframing our personal relationship with Jesus so as to remove the ankle weights and other superfluous stuff that he never intended for us to take on—the things that prevent us from enjoying the freedom and exhilaration of holding his hand as we walk through life. I know that a lot of us carry some baggage from our past church experiences; if we can let it go, we'll be all the lighter for the journey ahead.

3

Please Accept My Apology

You don't make progress by standing on the sidelines whimpering and complaining. You make progress by implementing ideas.
—**Shirley Chisholm**

Confession is good for the soul. And sometimes it requires eating a heaping slice of humble pie. As someone who has spent most of his life in full-time ministry—as a pastor, missions leader, and ministry worker—I know the reality of the systems, structures, words, and labels that have been built up around the organized church and missions organizations over the years. For centuries we've tried to engineer and shape a system that will provide love and care for our neighbors and discipleship for believers, all while spreading the gospel to all the nations of the world. I believe everything has been set up, changed, tweaked, torn down, and rebuilt time and again with the best of intentions; but I also believe that we have used human hands to organize and direct the mission of God, and with our human hands we often get so many things wrong.

If I could write a letter to my fellow Christians about the state of the church and its mission, it would go something like this:

LOVE CHILD

Dear fellow follower of Christ,

We got it wrong.

For centuries we have perpetuated certain ideas and teachings that are inconsistent with the grassroots truth of Christ.

You have within you the hope of the world. You have been lovingly made, and you are a strategic piece of the solution. You can't sit on the sidelines. God needs you as his missionary in the world.

The mission of healing requires us all. The mission to bring hope, the mission to bring peace, and the mission of love is in our hearts and needs our voice, our hands, and our feet. You only need to use what God has given you to take part in his mission in the world.

But as church and ministry leaders, we have too often failed you. We have focused on buildings more than community. We have focused on keeping you in rather than sending you out. And we have perpetuated a hierarchy that somehow made it seem that only pastors and missionaries were meant for full-life service to God's work in the world. For these errors, and so many others, we seek your forgiveness.

God's mission is for all believers. You can be used exactly as you have been formed and transformed. And while the Lord is working through you, he will keep transforming you.

Please Accept My Apology

With terms like *short-term mission* and *long-term mission*, we have framed God's mission as something which is less than full-life and full-time.

With the way we've used words like *calling*, we have framed God's call to join his mission as something for a few, as an "if," when really it's a "how," and for everyone.

And with terms like *mission field*, we have accidentally pretended that there may be places where we live our lives for God's mission and places where we don't.

Your mission field is the whole world—twenty-four hours a day and every day of the year. Your full life is required, and that's exactly what you promised when you told Jesus that you were joining his cause. If we failed to mention that, or to reinforce it, we have let you down.

Forgive us. Christians are God's missionary force, yet we've set up a system that treats missions as something for a few, when in fact it is God's call to all who seek to follow him.

Please accept our apology and work with us to change the way we organize, talk about, and live out Christianity and God's mission. You are known and loved by God exactly as you are. And you have the hope for your neighbors, your community, and the world living inside you.

Sincerely,
Geoff

LOVE CHILD

And while I'm confessing, let me also share that I've only come to these realizations in recent years. For nearly my entire life I have been actively involved in the church, yet I somehow missed the main gist of the story. I'm one of those people who thought that "others" were supposed to do the heavy lifting of Christian action. Indeed, I may have missed the entire point of inviting Christ into my life in the first place.

Like so many, I focused on the fact that Jesus died for my sins—that he loves me so much that he died in my place and for my transgressions. But I neglected to take it a step further and develop an understanding of *why* he did it. And now that I see the bigger picture, now that I know the full story, I can't help but see the holes in the teachings, the missing focus in praise songs, and the massive gulf between what we Christians have signed up for and what we actually do.

Over the last few years I've been on a listening journey with Christians around the world. Not just people who say they're Christians, but Scripture-quoting, faithful-church-attending, the-Bible-influences-me-every-day followers of Jesus. From Ghana to Hong Kong, and from Brazil to the United States, I've listened to groups across seven countries talk about what they think we Christians are supposed to be all about.

And you know what? I discovered that I was not alone in my misunderstanding of God's intention for us all. Most of the Christians I've talked to seem to be missing a *big* part of what being a Christian is all about.

Yes, Jesus died and rose from the grave to redeem you and me, to clear away the sin that keeps us from a relationship with the Father. This means we're free!

Please Accept My Apology

This means we're loved! This is the most incredible gift ever imagined by our Father and Creator.

But is that all?

Don't get me wrong; that's plenty—a gift that can never be outdone. But did God do it just so we could be reunited with him?

No, my friends, we have a greater purpose. We have a role in Creation. It requires living out Christ's love in real time, on the ground, wherever we are. It's not about shining brightly within our churches. It's about serving as lights in the darkness.

4

The Phantom and the Opera

We often miss hearing God's voice simply because we aren't paying attention.
— Rick Warren

Singing at church and in school as a child brought me a lot of joy.

I loved the way we strived to make our voices come together to create something beautiful. We were all separate, all important, and all working in unity for a greater good. Of course, in the greater context of my life choices, my love for music was incongruous. It was a strange and peaceful island, floating in a hot sea of angry defiance. Yet I knew to the core of my being that I belonged there. It was a soothing respite for my soul.

Between my church, school, and extracurricular choir directors, I had a lot of male role models in my life who were good, kind human beings whom I respected greatly. In other circumstances I would have rebuked their authority, yet these men were able to wield it artfully and render something beautiful. Their leadership brought people of varying heights, weights, IQs, and acne coverage together, uniting our voices into the kind of harmonious music that would make people weep. I admired this, and ultimately decided this would be my path.

LOVE CHILD

Mr. Earl was my high school choir director. He had thinning white hair, a wife named Connie, and an exceptional influence on my love for choral music. With Mr. Earl, we sang classical music, chamber music, and spirituals. He pushed us hard and had an ardent passion for pulling the very best out of us. Mr. Earl expected each choir to show up and give every practice our best effort, which sometimes added up to three or four choir practices a day. We were teenagers, so we would fill gaps, of course, with pranks and cajoling, all the while making fun of Mr. Earl's bald spot.

Mr. Earl was a graduate of Chapman University in Orange, California. He took us down to the campus a couple of times, and he invited the Chapman choir to come up to our school in Santa Rosa as well. Their program was amazing, and I desperately wanted to be part of it. My GPA and SAT scores certainly wouldn't open any doors for me, but my voice could. With Mr. Earl's help, I applied for and received a music scholarship to Chapman University. My double major: conducting and opera performance.

My life was about to change.

At Chapman I was suddenly protected from the winds that seemed to constantly create instability in my life. I had a room, access to a cafeteria, and a whole new group of people who were completely unaware of my past. Chapman's campus was the first place where I felt I could control my own choices. It was literally a ticket out of the chaos that was my childhood. The anger that had been my protective shield for eighteen years was no longer a necessary part of my armor. As it melted away, I invested in activities and clubs. A couple of friends and I started a fraternity, and I joined student government as the social director, which put me at the helm of our campus homecoming celebration and other major events.

And then there was Travis, my roommate. Travis was a football-playing surfer from just outside San Diego. He was athletic, he played the guitar, and he read his Bible every morning.

Faith was a topic we discussed regularly, because church was a familiar subject to me and I was intensely curious about his faith.

When Travis read his Bible, it was clearly not just for the stories. He was connecting with God. For Travis, this was a daily conversation with God—a chance to glean his wisdom and actually receive his direction. I remember one day he was sitting with his Bible open and seemed outwardly frustrated, even saying out loud, "Dang it!"

When I asked him what was wrong, he said, "I just can't figure out what God is trying to tell me."

His use of the present tense threw me. Travis was really trying to talk with God, not just read historical ideas and concepts. He viewed his Bible reading as an exchange—a two-way conversation.

I always knew God was real and I never really struggled with doubting his existence. But I had never developed a practice to understand the nature of God. I had never thought of investing in a tangible, everyday relationship with him. But Travis had. And it got my mind spinning.

Maybe God was more than just the "Him" in hymns. Maybe Jesus was more than a storyteller. Maybe in all my years at church, I had missed something huge. In fact, maybe I had missed the entire point. Maybe God wasn't who I thought he was.

LOVE CHILD

Travis was a big part of my aha moment regarding God. Clarity didn't come all at once, of course; but looking back, I see my time with Travis as a pivotal moment in my faith.

While the college "me" was transforming on multiple levels, and my social lifestyle was on the upswing, my grades followed a similar yet opposing arc. It became clear I needed to refocus my priorities on my academic life. So I buckled down, cut back on the fun stuff, and decided I would get my grades up. Of course, when I made that decision, I'd yet to step into Marjery Enix's Music Theory 3 class.

I thought Music Theory 3 was going to be like my other music classes, but I was so very wrong. To say it was painful doesn't do it justice. It was math, not music, and let's just say math has never been my friend.

Ms. Enix was just about the most brilliant and scattered professor I've ever had. She could digress to a side topic with great ease, and I regularly found myself treading water in the murky depths of harmonic overtones. I barely dragged myself to the music hall and up the long flight of stairs for class each day, and an epic personal battle ensued each night as I tried to force myself to attempt the homework back in my dorm room. By the time it was all over, I knew this class marked the curtain call on my dream of making music a career. I went to the dean and asked to be allowed to change my major but keep my music scholarship. Thankfully he agreed, as long as I continued singing in the choirs.

Around that time, I took a public relations ethics class and felt the seeds of a new passion take root. Morality was a foundational element to the curriculum; we covered classical theories of ethics, along with current events and case study analyses, while participating in vibrant classroom discussions on ethical behavior in the workplace. The class made me feel alive. It sparked something deep inside my soul, and I was hooked. I declared a new major: public relations.

At its surface, this choice of major may not seem ironic. But to me, looking back, it is entirely comical. How could someone with an earned reputation like mine—with scorched terrain spanning two states—say with a straight face that he should be in charge of managing other people's reputations?

The Public Relations Society of America defines public relations as a strategic communication process that builds mutually beneficial relationships between organizations and their publics.

Here's the problem: relationships weren't my thing. I mean relationships with deep roots were not something I had ever figured out. I managed a couple along the way (thank you, Katie and Matt), but I had never acquired a skill set to develop and nurture quality, lasting relationships. As a kid, I never stayed in one place or in one school long enough to make and maintain strong friends. In fact, I spent much of my childhood alone. In high school I jumped between crowds, doing enough to fit in with my respective choir or weekend group, but not figuring out how to forge the kind of relationships where today, as an adult, I might invite my old high school buddies over to watch the game. I guess it shouldn't be a surprise that I wasn't good at digging deep and building friendships that spanned beyond a shared interest like church, singing, or slashing tires. I had never learned.

I also think I probably wasn't motivated to do so. My dad hadn't shown up for me in any meaningful way and my mom got rid of me whenever times got tough.

And my teachers? I felt like all it took was a couple of tantrums and they'd be chomping at the bit to ship me off to be another school's problem.

I couldn't rely on others, so why invest in them? The only person I could count on was myself.

But this was changing. Travis had opened up a new possibility. Maybe there *was* someone out there who wanted a relationship with me. Maybe God wasn't a phantom Creator who hovered somewhere above—but not among—us.

I was beginning to see that Jesus wasn't simply a noble, moral, historical character like Gandhi or Rosa Parks. Throughout the chaos of my young life, God had always been there, waiting quietly for me to put the pieces together. Our Father is patient.

It might sound like I was slowly but surely getting my act together, and for a twenty-one-year-old kid in California, I was. I was moving forward in positive ways: rethinking my faith, recalibrating my work/play balance, rebuilding my GPA, and redefining my career goals. I was on a new journey. And I was bringing some baggage along for the ride.

5

Naked and Afraid

We seek out people who we hope will fix what our childhood broke.

—Yasmin Mogahed

My senior year of college, I got an internship with the County of Orange in the office of Community and Media Relations. My role was to help write press releases and coordinate the communication between outside media and our county representatives. Little did I know I was walking into a firestorm. Just prior to accepting the role, the county had declared the first municipal bankruptcy in US history. Needless to say, I was thrown into the deep end of the media pool and quickly had to figure out how my college learning translated into actual work.

While I was taking steps to build my professional life, I was making strides in my personal life too. Even though my path had changed dramatically in college—and I had been exercising new, relational muscles—I still felt very alone in the world. There was a deep need within me to find my lifelong partner. I wanted someone to walk with me.

I spent a lot of time thinking about my future, wondering what my life would look like. Who would I marry? Logically, I figured I should find *someone* to marry before I graduated. How would you even find a girl after college? Work would be a weird place, because if it didn't work out, well, that would be awkward. And besides, I was literally surrounded by cute girls at Chapman. The odds were in my favor! Of course, in hindsight, I now know that logic does not necessarily lead to love.

I started dating a girl whom I'd known as a friend for a couple of years. She was attractive, we had many friends in common, and we had both grown up in the church. Jackpot, right? After three quick months of dating we were engaged, and we got married about a year later. Two years after that, we had a son.

Marriage was a new concept to me. I didn't have any examples to learn from or emulate. We were a young couple trying to find our way based on books, prayers, ideas, and the knowledge that this thing we were doing was what God had designed. As we understood it, this was the formula for two young Christians to have a great life:

- ☑ Go to church
- ☑ Get married
- ☑ Have kids
- ☑ Work hard
- ☑ Try not to sin

We were doing our best to check all the boxes.

Upon graduation, I was offered a job at a top public relations firm in California. I was in my element! Our account roster included clients like Disney and many other large and incredible accounts. I'll never forget the day we spent together with the Disney folks brainstorming ideas around a new theme park. They had a wild idea to build something they were calling "California Adventure" on top of the guest parking lot at Disneyland.

Naked and Afraid

The whole meeting was a magical chaos of imagery, adjectives, and crazy ideas. Nothing was off the table. The conversation was much like what you'd hear from a room full of preschoolers. Our minds wandered aimlessly, and we all shared whatever we were thinking about, with no filters. After a few hours the Disney team leader said, "Thanks! This was great!" and left. Was this really my job? It was a dream.

About a year into the role I started working with a new client who wanted to do a sort of lottery promotion to help raise their public image. The idea was that the one-hundred thousandth customer would win a big prize, and the company would then tell the story of this customer and how they used their product to make their life better. It's a common tactic to generate good stories about a product in the press by creating an opportunity for a very public customer endorsement.

I was the junior associate on the account, but I was given a lot of responsibility to make sure we performed well for the client. After many weeks of planning, the magic day approached. Our plans were about to spin into gear. As the office buzz around this initiative grew louder, I started to pick up on some conversations that our senior associate was having with the client. It sounded like maybe instead of picking the actual one-hundred thousandth customer, we were going to be gathering background details and interviews from fifteen to twenty customers who were all "around the one-hundred thousandth customer" and then declaring the one with the best story to be the winner.

An internal conflict started brewing inside of me. I was dealing with a visceral rub between my professional responsibilities and something deep in my soul.

The very same day I was called into the senior partner's office for a meeting. "As you know," he said, "one of the senior account managers is leaving, and so a spot has opened up. We're impressed with your work, and we'd like to offer you the promotion. If you're interested, you'd start the new job next week."

It was amazing! A senior-level promotion at my dream job! I was certainly going places now! A massive feeling of confidence surged over me as I heard myself say, "Thank you, I'm really honored. I wonder, though, if you could help me understand something about one of the accounts I'm currently working on which seems like it might be ethically questionable."

"Sure thing," he replied. "What's your question?"

I explained the lottery promotion and what I thought I had overheard. Without missing a beat, he replied, "Yup, that's all correct. That's the strategy."

Huh? Not what I was expecting to hear. My mind was spinning, so I asked him if it would be alright for me to take a day to think and pray about the promotion, explaining that I didn't want to say yes if perhaps I'd be uncomfortable down the road.

"I'll tell you what," he said. "How about we make Friday your last day?"

I was shell-shocked. Just minutes after being offered a big promotion, I was fired. Had I done the right thing? Or was I incredibly naïve and stupid?

I walked back to my desk and opened up my Yahoo browser. In the search bar, I entered "religious communications." If my faith had just cost me my job, I decided I'd save myself the trouble of going through it again and instead work for an organization where morality was central to its mission.

Upon reflection, I see that this very brief conversation and my resultant internet search were a huge pivot point for me. While my boss decided my fate, I had put the wheels in motion by voicing my concerns. It was a reflexive conversation—one that didn't require much thinking. I believe that's because I already knew that staying true to my beliefs was more important to me than the opportunity to wield my own expense account as I wined and dined big clients at the best restaurants. So when I was faced with the ultimatum of honoring God or enjoying a good gig that compromised my morals, I didn't have to consider whether or not I should speak up. I knew what I had to do.

Taking the time to really consider your values and beliefs ahead of time so you're not forced to make snap decisions in the heat of the moment is an important part of your spiritual development. You have to honestly and earnestly consider: Who are you and who are you going to serve? Are you going to make decisions that serve your own interests, or God's?

At some point we're all faced with this decision. We have to look at the work we're doing and the skills we've been given, and we must decide if we're going to intentionally use it all to build bridges within the world, or if we are content living compartmentalized lives, where our work and church lives are on separate tracks that only intersect when it's convenient or comfortable. Both scenarios have consequences.

After my firing, I ended up finding an agency that helped churches use data and insights about the people and communities around them so they could reach people more effectively. They didn't actually have an opening when I first reached out. But the president of the firm recognized the name of the PR firm I was coming from and wanted to create a job. They paid me to sit tight and not look for other jobs while they got everything squared away to hire me and give me office space. The magnitude of this turn of events was not lost on me.

For my new role, I was responsible for presenting demographic information for strategy planning purposes to large groups of highly regarded ministers. We provided a popular and effective service to churches and denominations around the country. Seminaries certainly weren't teaching students how to access and interpret data about their surrounding communities so they could touch the hearts and minds of people better. This information was all new to them. And so at the age of twenty two I found myself part of a small company that was helping more than seventy-five thousand churches in the United States.

More than once before a presentation, I was struck by imposter syndrome. I felt too young and too inexperienced to be telling these great spiritual leaders what to do and how to expand the impact of their churches. I was just a kid who came from nothing. I didn't have any great spiritual legacy that earned me the right to lead these great men and women. I felt like a fraud. And yet pastors, priests, bishops, and ministers from over a dozen major denominations kept coming to my sessions and leaving with notes and plans for action.

Of course, in hindsight I can appreciate that this is exactly where God wanted me. But at times I felt so inadequate and ill-equipped. I think this is a really common struggle for people. In fact, maybe it's something you bump up against too. Instead of staying focused on what we know to be true, we allow ourselves to be bombarded by self-doubt as we measure ourselves against worldly standards. It's so easy to fall into that trap. But I'm pretty sure God doesn't care how old we are, how credentialed we are, how athletic we are, or how impressive our resumes are. He just wants us to use our talents for his mission. That's it. He'd like us to willingly put our passions and skills to use for his work and purpose.

Throughout this time, I learned a lot about myself and about my faith. After five years with the firm, and five more years doing the same work under my own company, I had earned an MBA, traveled to all but two of the fifty states, connected with thousands of pastors and ministry leaders, and savored great stories about new ministries being formed to serve people all over the country. I had also taken a deep dive into missiology—the study of missions. I co-facilitated leadership development workshops for pastors with Alan Roxburgh, a brilliant guy who has written books on missiology, change, and something called liminality, which I've come to appreciate as the basic state of Christians within the continuum of time and space. No, seriously! Look it up!

Alan is one of those people who operates on a different plane than the rest of us, and I learned a ton while we were traveling and teaching together. He introduced me to something called *The Gospel and our Culture Network*, which led to more books and more studying about the true nature of the church and Christ's mission in the world.

After years of being in the church, working for the church, and learning about the original heartbeat of the church, I was becoming more keenly aware of a bigger, more glorious picture of our role here on earth, much like when you stand very close—almost nose-to-canvas—with an impressionist painting. When your focus is small, you see individual brushstrokes. But when you slowly back up, you're able to take in the whole masterpiece.

My work and life experience were casting light on why we are all here, and at the same time it was exposing some flaws within the approach taken by the Christian church. I was starting to see a deep, fundamental issue. The more pastors and church leaders I met with, the more I could see it. In fact, it got to the point that I couldn't unsee it.

No matter how much time, energy, planning, and strategizing church leaders spent on understanding who was in their community and how these people could be reached, it didn't translate into an outwardly focused church body. I realized this was because the people who attended church didn't see themselves as part of God's workforce. I mean, they would participate in events and outreach, but in terms of redesigning their whole lives around God's mission, that wasn't happening. In fact, it was almost unheard of for the average person.

Christians love God. We love his heart for the lost and suffering. We love the hope offered through redemption in Jesus. We love serving and being part of a faith community.

We also love handing the day-to-day work off to someone else.

6

Checkmate

Chess is rarely a game of ideal moves. Almost always, a player faces a series of difficult consequences whichever move he makes.
—DAVID SHENK

As my career was yielding growth and promise, it was becoming clear that something was dying in my marriage.

A few years ago, my pastor said the church has done a great job of telling youth that marriage is what God intended for true intimacy, sex, and lifelong companionship, but the church has done a horrible job of helping young adults understand how to build a Christ-centered marriage and what God's love really looks like within the context of a husband-wife relationship. My wife and I clearly had a lot in common, and we loved each other in our way, but I'm not sure that either of us really understood the core tenets of a relationship built on God's love.

After about five years of marriage, we were clearly struggling to connect. My work travel schedule slowly started to shift from something that fueled my desire to serve the church to something that helped me escape from home. We made up what we thought a marriage was supposed to be, read books, prayed, journaled, and sought advice and guidance from pastoral and secular counselors; but what we made up was different than what

God designed, and that truth was becoming more and more clear as time went on.

At least my business was going well. That is, until 2008. Suddenly contracts stopped coming in. It was a common story for many small business owners that year. The downturn of the US financial markets impacted church giving, which impacted church spending, which resulted in my business finances falling off a cliff. I was forced to close up shop.

Both my work life and my home life were not just indicating stress fractures; they were clearly broken. First things first: I needed work to feed the family. Thankfully, my career had afforded me a large network, and within a few months I was invited to pastor the second campus of a two-thousand-member church.

I took the job and served the church for three years. On my first Sunday, the congregation at our campus was very small, with just eighty-five people. But we grew exponentially, and over time we developed a strong, healthy, outward-focused community.

The approach was simple really: we encouraged people to step into their gifts and passions for kingdom purposes, and provided the support of our community along the way. If a congregation member came to me with an idea, and they wanted to lead it, we celebrated it and even provided space and some funds, if we could, to help get it rolling. We ended up launching a couple of drama groups that did performances for the community, a café, countless small groups, worship bands of varying styles, and eventually even started finding space for other community groups as well. We did almost anything we could do to keep the congregation's focus outside of the church, while using the body to sustain each other and our efforts for the journey.

Checkmate

Throughout my time as a pastor, I learned that getting people to do what they are passionate about, for the kingdom, is mostly a matter of encouraging them and not letting church committees or others create needless roadblocks. Of course, we all got some things right and some things wrong. We knew we would. We celebrated missteps as an opportunity for course correction, because our main goal was *not* looking for great numbers or big results, although those were wonderful when they happened. Our main goal was to get believers off their butts and out into the world for Christ. In other words, we weren't focused on the impact of the outreach or ministry, but rather the heart of the person who was stepping out for Christ.

I think that is worth underscoring: we were not focused on impact. Too often, churches and Christians alike judge God's work using man's measures. For example, "I'm going to have a conversation with Jack *so that* he has a chance to become a believer."

I think this is a common mindset, but it's fatally flawed because it makes us humans believe that *we* are in charge of the outcome. We're not. By having a talk with Jack, we are obeying God's direction to love our neighbor. Sharing his love is the most loving thing we can do. Whether or not Jack chooses to follow Jesus is out of our hands and in God's hands.

When we focus on our own obedience rather than the outcome of our actions, we keep God where he belongs—on the throne—and avoid putting ourselves there in his place. Equally important, when God speaks and we not only listen but act on his prompting, that's when we grow in relationship with him. We get better and better at hearing his voice. Of course, if something great comes of it, that's awesome. But it's not our call whether or not we should act based on how impactful we think our action will be. That's God's call to make.

Our Palm Sunday service was one of my favorite services of the year. We called it U2charist. The bands did covers of U2 songs, the message was all about missions involvement locally and globally, and at the end of the service everyone would go out into the foyer with instructions to sign up with two or three of the community or mission groups that had set up tables. We had groups from local homeless ministries, elder care ministries, and global opportunities like Compassion International and the ONE Campaign. Each year, the U2charist services drew crowds of 1,200 or more for the weekend. We even gave out glow sticks for people to wave, because a bunch of people flicking their lighters inside the worship space seemed like a bad idea.

It was through these U2charist events that God moved me onward toward the next milestone in my journey by introducing me to Compassion International. After one of the services, I got to chatting with a guy named Brad who was the representative at the Compassion table. Brad wasn't just a volunteer; he worked for Compassion and encouraged me to apply. After my initial application, a few interviews, and several months of waiting, I was asked to join Compassion's marketing team.

As you may know, Compassion International is a ministry focused on releasing children from poverty, in Jesus' name, all around the world. People like you and me get to sponsor a child and help make sure he or she stays healthy, has a good education, and a jump start toward the life God intended. Most people think child sponsorship is all about what you do for the child, but the transformation goes both ways—that's the way God works.

I had the privilege of serving at Compassion for seven years, first as marketing director for intervention programs like clean water, malaria, HIV/AIDS, and disaster response, and later developing new fundraising products and new ways to engage Christians with our ministry.

With the exception of my first job at the PR agency, all of my work up to that point had been focused around God's mission and ministry. While I had soaked up a lot of knowledge about missions along the way, I was driven to learn more. Compassion offered tuition assistance to employees, so I enrolled at Fuller Seminary to pursue a doctorate in missiology and intercultural studies. My early passion for understanding audiences and data and faith had evolved. I wanted to understand catalysts for and dynamics behind spiritual development and how the mission of the Christian church is advanced by those of us who follow Jesus.

Sometimes I think about my journey with God as a game of chess with a master chess coach. I make one move, he makes another. Of course, he always wins. Always. Because he can see ten, fifty, one hundred, thousands of moves ahead, while I'm usually not able to see much farther than the end of my nose. Yet if I were to give up and walk away from the board, I'd stop learning from him. I wouldn't see the moves he makes and get better at hearing his voice to guide my own moves.

Jumping into the doctoral program at Fuller seemed like a natural move for me—but I didn't see all the pieces on the board. Over the next few years, what I thought was forward momentum would slowly crumble. I was losing one match after another. I felt defeated.

It started with my divorce. After years of counseling, retreats, Bible study, prayers, and trying, trying, trying, my marriage ended. It became very clear to me that whatever "this" was, it was not what God had intended for marriage. I was devastated and emotionally depleted.

I was also un-friended. As word began to spread about my divorce, friends began to disappear. Some quietly, some with loud, judgmental announcements. Divorce is a sin, I was a sinner, and therefore, apparently, I was no longer worthy of connecting with many friends and coworkers.

Once again I was labeled with scandal. Once again the religious elite were whispering and casting me aside. It was unjust, yet at my weakest moments I believed I deserved to be treated like a leper. So I threw myself further into my job, drowning my pain in productivity.

Then came the layoff. As part of a workforce reduction, my role at Compassion International came to an abrupt halt. It was incredibly sudden, and worse yet I was out of the country when the news was released. Needless to say, the flight home was very long. I wish I could say I saw it coming—that I had steeled my heart and my resolve for this blow. But I hadn't.

Beyond the obvious implications when one loses a job, I also realized this would mean my doctoral work would thereby halt. I could not afford to continue my studies at Fuller.

Suddenly I found myself with no wife and no job. I was a seminary dropout and I had fewer friends. Even my son was only with me half-time. I was alone again. It was strange and depressing and yet so familiar.

Checkmate

While the downward spiral of my marriage over the years had been lonely, I wasn't living in isolation. I was still part of a family unit, albeit an unhealthy one. Now I was a full-time divorcee and a part-time parent. I was untethered, at the whims of where the wind chose to take me. For someone so determined to change his childhood trajectory—someone so focused on building a stable marriage with a solid partner and a life absent of volatility and insecurity—this was a failure of cataclysmic and truly devastating proportions.

How could I have let this happen? How could I have allowed this to be my son's new life? Was Mason going to grow up feeling unsettled and unrooted as he bounced between his mom and me? Would he question our love for him? The potential parallels to my own childhood pressed hard on my shoulders. Amid the darkness, I felt history was repeating itself, leaving me awash in shame. This was a failure I did not want to own. All I had ever wanted was someone that I could trust with all my heart, someone who would be there for me no matter what. Now I was alone, exposed to the elements with no cover and no one to cling to.

At this point I closed the blinds on my heart and my apartment. I was numb with grief. I mindlessly watched Netflix and then swung to the opposite end of the spectrum, working out to complete exhaustion at the gym.

What was I?

Who was I?

My identity had always been intertwined with my job, and my status as a husband and father. But now I was gripped by fear—fear that I would always be alone, fear that I wouldn't heal from this pain, fear that I was a failure. I was living a life that I did not want. I was bruised and battered, a shell of my former self. I couldn't see God's plan in any of this. And I certainly didn't feel like I deserved any of it. I was lost. I needed to reconnect with my Father.

As part of my layoff from Compassion, I had received severance pay. Instead of tucking it away in the bank as preparation for my unpaid job search ahead, I did something that probably didn't make sense to people. I took the money and went to the UK for a weeklong spiritual retreat. I was desperate to recenter and hear God's voice again. And I had to find my voice with him, as well. I wanted to understand how to reengage our game. I needed to learn from the Master.

In *The Screwtape Letters*, by C. S. Lewis, senior demon Screwtape writes letters of advice to his demon nephew, Wormwood, who is charged with tempting a human toward Satan. In one passage Screwtape tells Wormwood that nothing is more dangerous to Satan than when a human has been abandoned, yet still obeys God.

The retreat I chose was run by the Northumbria Community in the north of England, just south of the Scottish wall. For many years I'd been using their Rule of Life for my daily prayers, so it seemed only natural that at this time, which was perhaps the lowest in my life, I should go to the mother ship—or as they call it, the "Mother House."

As part of daily life at the retreat, we observed the Rule of Life and prayed four times each day: morning, noon, evening, and bedtime. It was a time of peace and great quiet. Each evening after the Compline reading, the resident members of the order and all of us retreat participants would sit in silence. The first night it was an uncomfortable silence, but soon I began to crave it. The silence began to feel full and deep, as if the presence of God was right there with us. Soon no one wanted to leave.

Checkmate

Some nights we'd sit for hours, and then one by one we'd get up and quietly go to our rooms.

First Kings 19 records the time when Elijah was at the end of his rope after a particularly gruesome run-in with the prophets of Baal. He was beyond exhausted and needed refreshing from God. Elijah walked forty days and nights to Horeb, "the mountain of God," where he went into a cave and spent the night.

He received word to "Go out and stand on the mountain in the presence of the LORD, for the LORD is about to pass by" (v. 11). From inside the cave, Elijah saw and heard a mighty wind, then an earthquake, and finally a fire. "And after the fire came a gentle whisper. When Elijah heard it, he pulled his cloak over his face and went out and stood at the mouth of the cave" (vv. 12–13). Then the Lord spoke to Elijah, giving him the direction and encouragement he desperately needed.

The silence of those nights in England nudged me to reflect on this story. I wasn't facing crushing winds, or an earthquake, or a fire, but I had experienced a divorce, severed friendships, and a layoff, all of which wreaked what felt like irreparable damage upon my heart. Elijah knew that he wasn't going to find a connection with God amid the destruction. There just wasn't any way to hear God's voice through the chaos. But like Elijah, I was on the other side of the storm, and I could once again hear the Lord's gentle whisper.

When I returned home, I walked the prayer labyrinth at a local church each day while I prayed. I suddenly had no other distractions, and because I was unemployed, I had lots of time. I had an overwhelming desire to build a deeper relationship with the only Father I'd ever really known.

7

Let's Talk

Communication to a relationship is like oxygen to life. Without it ... it dies!
—Tony A. Gaskins Jr.

Learning how to open up and talk with God through unscripted, free-form prayer has not always been easy for me. In fact, it was a huge struggle for me as a young adult. Growing up in the Episcopal Church, prayer was a regular part of every service. But the lion's share of it was prewritten.

Priest: Bless the Lord who forgives all our sins.
People: His mercy endures forever.

They were common prayers that we recited out loud, as one voice, in an act of unity as believers. The prayers are etched into my memory banks and are a cherished part of my prayer life. As a child, they made me feel like I belonged to something. Even though we may have been strangers in a new town, my mom and I knew when to pray and when to pause, when to listen and when to respond. The Episcopalian prayer tradition always felt like home to me.

Nonetheless, developing a comfort level with the more casual, spur-of-the-moment type of prayer is important too, because it reveals what's on your heart. My mother was a great role model for this type of prayer. It was something that I saw her do every day throughout my childhood. She was a devoted champion and believer in praying for others in need. I admired this in her—and still do—but for me, this wasn't a practice that came naturally. I think it's because my view of God as the high, holy Creator of the universe didn't align with a casual, heartfelt chat.

A lot of my friends know Jesus as their friend and have no trouble engaging in spontaneous, conversational prayer with him. Many of them, though, have had to learn the reverence part. They almost forget that he is the Lord, our holy Redeemer.

For me it was the opposite. I was so entrenched in the mindset that God is to be exalted and praised that I struggled with what to say to him in unscripted prayer. To get better at this, I had to make an intentional effort to expand my reflexive view of God so that it embraced the whole Trinity—Father, Son, and Holy Spirit. And if I truly wanted to deepen the roots of my relationship with the Lord, I needed to start talking.

When I first started saying my own prayers, I was pretty uncomfortable. I still felt like I was approaching a throne so golden that I wasn't worthy, even though I knew in my heart that I had been invited. This most holy vision inherently made my approach more formal, with each word carefully selected. I didn't want to offend God or say something irreverent. It was a genuine struggle to relax and open up, lifting the lid on my deepest fears and hurts, along with my praise and gratitude. But as with any worthwhile relationship, I invested. And over time my words started to flow more comfortably.

I prayed while I was biking and I prayed while I was mowing the lawn. I prayed silently and I prayed audibly. I prayed about the big stuff and I prayed about the mundane.

My prayer life now is an ongoing conversation throughout the day, in my thoughts and through my voice. It can take the form of questions, aggression, sorrow, concern, joy, and pure thankfulness. I've found that the more I talk with God, the easier it is to be honest, and the things that are genuinely on my heart are the things that come out.

These "living prayers" also work to intertwine my heart with God's heart. When I'm most connected with him, I am most sensitive to his love, guidance, and prompting. I am saddened by what surely saddens him, and I'm motivated to act in circumstances that are calling for a servant. I yearn to help those desperate for the comforting touch of Jesus. Prayer is the cord that binds me to his mission—and therefore my purpose—on earth.

Conversing regularly with God is like oxygen for me. I don't just want it, I need it. Like any worthwhile relationship, if I want my connection with God to grow, I have to invest in it.

You don't get closer to friends by saying hi every now and again and bumping into them at parties on the weekends. You spend time together, one-on-one. You take the time to talk, just the two of you. You ask questions, you actively listen, and you unabashedly pour out your heart, even though it makes you vulnerable.

Good relationships require honesty and strong relationships require trust, but across the board, the relationships you value most require time.

Opening up every nook and cranny of my heart to God and incorporating him into my everyday life has made my relationship with him and my understanding of his heart so natural. Like a best friend, when I'm sad, I turn to him for advice. When I'm happy, I turn to him to give thanks. When I'm worried or confused, I turn to him for guidance, prompting, and peace.

These ongoing conversations with God work for you, for me, and for his plan. Our prayers matter, often in unexplainable ways.

One example of this is the mysterious drawing of souls to God. Currently there is a historically unprecedented, widely documented, global movement of Muslims coming to faith in Christ. These conversions are happening throughout the Muslim world, and they are often spurred by dreams.

In the Muslim faith, considerable importance is attached to dreams. They are viewed as having a special authority. Muslims believe dreams should be taken seriously as they communicate truth, offering a unique view into the will of Allah.

That's why it is fascinating that countless stories shared by former Muslims include a dream about Jesus (known as Isa in Islam), glowing brightly, reaching out to them in love. Sometimes he has scars on his hands and sometimes he's holding a Bible—extending it toward them, inviting them to read it. They wake up knowing they should follow him.

In his book *A Wind in the House of Islam*, David Garrison traveled a quarter of a million miles from West Africa through Indonesia to interview more than one thousand former Muslims about how they came to faith in Jesus. Over and over again, he heard stories about these dreams. When people would reference the bright, glowing figure of Jesus in their dreams, David would often show them Matthew's account of the Transfiguration, which says that Jesus' "face shone like the sun, and his clothes became as white as the light" (Matt 17:2). The people responded with elation as they acknowledged this was the figure of their dreams.

I believe this movement of Muslims coming to Christ is no accident. For decades Christians have been praying for Muslims, specifically that God would reveal himself to them through dreams.

The annual *30 Days of Prayer for the Muslim World* likely involves more Christians in prayer than any other event or campaign. It started back in 1992, when a group of missions leaders were praying at a meeting in the Middle East. These leaders were convicted about their attitudes toward the Muslim world, and they committed to becoming more intentional in demonstrating God's love for Muslim people. The *30 Days of Prayer* movement was born in an effort to bring Christians together to learn about and pray for Muslims all over the world.

I have taken part in *30 Days of Prayer* and have prayed for Muslims throughout the month of Ramadan. Our collective prayers are that as Muslims are seeking God intensely during Ramadan, he would reveal himself in a new way. We pray they would understand that the Jesus they see as a holy man is really the Son of God, the One who came for them. We pray that they would have dreams of who Christ is, and that they would have visions of Jesus.

I know to my core that prayers work and the Holy Spirit is active. Jesus said, "The wind blows wherever it pleases. You hear its sound, but you cannot tell where it comes from or where it is going" (John 3:8). This is the Holy Spirit, bringing the love of Jesus to every corner of the world through divine encounters—even absent of a Jesus follower to begin a person's quest.

LOVE CHILD

Prayer involves action. Praying for those who don't know God is important work. Praying for our neighbors, for our communities, for the lost and forgotten … this is vital. Of course, we also pray for ourselves and our families. I remember going for a long walk when I was desperate for healing. I was so angry about my life that I yelled, screaming at God with tears streaming down my face. If anyone had seen me, they would have thought I lost my mind.

Prayer brings comfort—God brings comfort. But prayer is only part of the equation. Action must follow.

8

Getting Served by Miss Addie

Yesterday's gone and tomorrow is blind, so I live one day at a time.
—**Willie Nelson**, "One Day at a Time"

When I was in my twenties and living in Southern California, I served as the music director at a small United Methodist church in a beautiful beachside community. The town was a destination along the Pacific Coast Highway … a place where couples strolled along the palm-lined boardwalk, the golf course was dotted with sherbet-colored polo shirts, and people were known for having mellow, down-to-earth dispositions even though their address was anchored by a trendy SoCal zip code.

Our church choir was primarily populated with retirees—a mix of native Californians and transplants from the Rocky Mountains through the Bible Belt. One of my favorite members of the choir was a woman in her late seventies named Miss Addie. Miss Addie was a sweet-tea sipping truth teller with a Southern accent. She had no problem telling you what's what, although she'd do it in a drawl so charming that you almost didn't realize you had just been set straight!

LOVE CHILD

At choir rehearsal one day, Miss Addie announced that the local soup kitchen and homeless shelter needed people to serve. "Since we're retired, and have time on our hands, we're the people to do it!" she said brightly. Miss Addie promptly pulled a clipboard out from her handbag. On it was attached a preprinted chart with instructions for folks to add their names and contact numbers for the time slots when they were available. Miss Addie handed the clipboard to the first soprano in the front row as she said, "We can make sure the homeless folks get their meals and we can help out this local charity too!"

The clipboard passed rapidly down the row without pause and without the pen touching paper even once. As the clipboard was handed back to the next row, Miss Addie said, "Excuse me, people, have we forgotten how to write down our names?"

The woman holding the hot potato said, "You know, Miss Addie, this is a great opportunity, but my husband and I moved here to retire. This is not really the type of activity that we do anymore. We like to serve, but now we do it in different ways. We've been serving all our lives. It's time for us."

Miss Addie cast her eyes along the row of sopranos who had just chosen not to add their signatures and said, "Well, I figure that if the good Lord thought I was done, then I'd be done! But as long as I'm still on this earth, sucking his air, it must be for his purpose."

I still remember the sting of her indignation, wondering if the looks on the faces of the choir were a product of guilt or self-reflection or both. Either way, Miss Addie's statement was worthy of consideration. It's still worthy today.

Getting Served by Miss Addie

Have you thought about why you're still sucking air? Do you think about why you're alive and what God's purpose might be for you on this earth? I think about that a lot. I've got to believe that every single aspect of my journey—from my work roles and personal relationships to my hopes and my hurts—can be used by God. He knows how my hardest lessons eventually transformed deep wounds into soft spots that have the potential to provide comfort to others who are in pain. God sees how my faith-filled, yet incredibly unstable upbringing, created in me a desire to cling fiercely to him—our Father who never leaves us. He witnesses how my past mistakes and missteps inform my path as I try to do a little better each and every day.

I know some people look back on their past with a sense of shame. I've definitely experienced that myself. It's a really heavy, uncomfortable existence. But we don't have to live that way.

God's forgiveness is pure and cleansing. It's light that slices through your darkness. And with time, it will gently wash away the sting from regrets that burn so deep you can't remember life before them. It will relieve the pains that paralyze—the types of pain that tell you you're not worthy of much, if anything.

Not only can he calm your pain and hurt, he can use it—all of it. I know this to the core of my being. My broken past—your broken past—makes God's glory shine even brighter to those around us.

But to be used by God, we must value community and the greater good. If we don't actually view the people around us and around the world as brothers and sisters in God's family, it's very difficult for us to make a deep, true sacrifice on their behalf. We should not just love those who love us back. We must love others because they exist. Because God created them and each one is precious in His sight.

To effectively serve God, we also need to surrender our lives daily to him. We need to regularly, intentionally invite him to take control, relinquishing our grip on creating our own stories and giving God full authorship. He's waiting for the invitation because he's not a thief; he won't steal our lives from us while we're watching Netflix or cooking dinner. We need to hand our lives over to him, and then be open and willing to go where he wants us to go.

Back in Southern California, Miss Addie reminded me and everyone else that there's no such thing as retirement in the kingdom of God. Your brothers and sisters are waiting, and your unique passions, skills, and abilities can and should be used for his purpose. If you can serve, you should serve. And as I've come to learn personally, through service and obedience you'll discover a holy contentment marked by joy and freedom and peace.

Miss Addie's clipboard chart ended up getting filled that day.

9

Take It Out of the Box

Just Do It.
—**Donald Katz**,
Just Do It: The Nike Spirit in the Corporate World

I have a friend from South Africa named Renette. She's the kind of friend who will tell you if there's something dangling out of your nose or if you have parsley in your teeth. She's very direct, and I really appreciate that about her. Renette doesn't dip her toe gingerly in any issue. She jumps in, assesses the situation, generates an opinion, and shares it without disclaimers or apologies or any emotional "extras" attached. She's a straight shooter whose observation skills are finely tuned.

One Christmas, Renette was visiting a friend and her family in Canada. While a houseguest with the family, she said her friend's father ordered a really nice, new smart TV. He waited for it to arrive, asking each member of the family—and Renette—every day if there had been a delivery or a phone call about an impending delivery.

Finally, after a full week, the TV was delivered. He was thrilled, and promptly slid the big new box into a clean spot in the garage.

After a few days, Renette asked him if she could help him install it. He declined, saying he was waiting for his son-in-law to come over and help. A week later, the new

TV still sat in its box in the garage. In the meantime, the family and Renette continued watching shows on the old TV that had bad sound and a screen that was covered in vertical stripes.

Two weeks AD (after delivery), the family was watching a hockey game on the old TV and someone casually, maybe cautiously, asked where the new TV was. Renette's friend explained that her father was waiting for his son-in-law to help install it. "But Dad," one of the kids said, "the TV has a stand. We can use it while you wait for it to be mounted on the wall."

The father looked perplexed and disappointed. He hadn't realized that the TV came with a stand. He could have been using it for the past two weeks.

Within the hour, the new TV was on the stand in all its glory, delivering a picture and sound unlike anything the family had experienced before.

Renette told me that as she reflected on this experience, she was struck by the parallels to the Christian faith.

The church shares the good news of Jesus and people are so happy to receive it. They accept it, celebrate it, and get excited about the prospects of using it, but don't really know how to, so they leave it in a box, stored in the garage.

Renette's analogy is brilliant. Churches have definitely not excelled at teaching Christians what to do with our faith. You don't need a theology degree or the results from a spiritual gifts survey to share the gospel. It's not as complicated as that. It comes with its own stand! To get started, all it takes is a simple act of love, like saying "hello" to your neighbor.

For Christians, I think sharing God's love should be like swimming is to a fish. Once we've opted into this new life, as a new creation, passing on the love of Christ should be second nature, a basic requirement like food or water that brings continued growth.

If churches could simply help Christians understand how easy it is to take the gospel out of the box, the world would be a different place.

But instead of teaching Christians how to share the love of Christ, I think if you were to ask most people—especially those who don't attend church very often, if at all—the church is about identification, not education. In fact, many churches seem to spend a lot of time and effort clearly and sometimes loudly defining what makes them different from the church down the road or across town.

For the most part, the span of denominations that we have today is the result of one group of Christians believing another group is flat-out wrong in their interpretation of the Bible, or how to worship, or some other mechanics of the Christian faith. And while I think digging into Scripture to seek God's truth is a valuable practice, I believe that generations of digging has created churches and denominations that are known by the deep moats that surround them, not the Maker who created them. It's hard to multiply God's kingdom when you're focused on dividing it.

People in church circles and even the greater community can often tell you which congregation supports same-sex marriage and which one ordains women, which one only worships with Wesleyan hymns and which one will collectively clutch its pearls if a member is seen buying a bottle of wine at the liquor store.

That reminds me of a joke I once heard:

> Why should you always take two Baptists when you go fishing?
>
> Because if you only take one, he'll drink all your beer.

For the record, I love Baptists. Here's another one for my fellow Anglican friends:

> What do you always find where three or four Anglicans are gathered?
>
> A FIFTH.

The trouble with our loudly articulated social stances, our politically based pulpit pounding, and our well-defined property lines is that they don't introduce people to Jesus. I mean, they might serve to initially draw people in if the church's principles align with that of the individual. Under that arrangement, however, they are connected by an idea or a belief or a perspective. Jesus isn't in the lead.

I think many of us have experienced the picket-sign-wielding college student asserting how Jesus would vote in the upcoming election or what God thinks about a proposed constitutional amendment. Do you think the student and all his energetic hooting and hollering have ever convinced anyone to switch sides? I don't either. But this isn't really a surprise, is it? I think we already know that impassioned arguments about who God loves and who he doesn't, who God has chosen and who he hasn't, who is right and who is wrong ... these things don't draw people to Jesus. People whose lives reflect Christ's love do.

So what happened? Why have so many churches chosen to take this path, differentiating themselves with such fervor—and sometimes even with glee? I think the number-one factor has been our own inability to see how the evil one can distract, substitute, and encourage us to focus on any number of topics except those which ultimately are most likely to introduce people to Jesus and grow the kingdom of God.

I know a guy named Palin who gets this. Palin and his wife work in Southeast Asia, where a significant part of Palin's role involves helping Jesus followers avoid imposing cultural aspects of Christianity upon other believers and attaching unnecessary baggage to biblical principles.

"The gospel will look different in every culture," said Palin. "Forcing a Western version of Christianity on others could very well repel potential believers."

For example, Palin started a church that has adapted to the local culture by imitating the 24/7 style of prayer common in the Hindu temples, providing opportunities for seekers to come at any time of the day or night to pray and converse over a cup of tea.

According to Palin, Jesus and the church are not bound by any cultural or religious labels, not even the label of "Christian." Palin says, "There is no Christian food, there is no Christian dress, there is no Christian wedding. ... You can sit on elephants and get married for all I care. It's about Jesus in your heart."

Palin understands that he—we—should share Jesus, not our culture or systems or statements or faith rituals. Yet still, we Christians often feel most comfortable when the God we worship is a God of our own design and construct, made in our own image. But this begs the question: Who, then, are we really worshipping?

10

The Tools of the Trade

The best way to find yourself is to lose yourself in the service of others.

—**Mahatma Gandhi**

According to the Canadian Red Cross, if you have food in the refrigerator, clothes on your back, a roof over your head, and a place to sleep, you are richer than 75 percent of the rest of the world. If you have money in the bank, in your wallet, and spare change in a dish somewhere, you are among the top 8 percent of the world's wealthy.[5]

These statistics describe me, and I'm willing to bet they describe you too. Compared to the majority of the world, we are immensely wealthy. All I have to do is look around me and I know this to be true. I have a home, a car, and clothes—clothes for work, for the weekend, and for exercising. As I cast my eyes along the kitchen counter where I'm working, I see a vase of flowers, post-it notes, magazines, books, a coffee mug, and three sprinkler heads for my weekend project. I am incredibly fortunate.

I also know these things are mostly just possessions. Yes, food sustains us, and shelter protects us. But objects … possessions … they're just things. While they may bring us some initial excitement or sense of self-gratification, those feelings are fleeting.

LOVE CHILD

To be sure, once the crisp coat of paint on the kitchen cabinets gets a few dings and the novelty of our new cappuccino machine wears away, many of us develop amnesia, forgetting that these things once brought us great joy. Quite often, the fix lies in heading back to our favorite shop or online retailer to boost our serotonin levels and restore our happiness.

The thing is, most of us know better than to get sucked into this cycle. We know in our hearts that transformation can't be bought. We know it's not on a shelf, or ready-to-ship, or on the showroom floor. We know transformation happens when we work on the invisible, intangible things of life—when we love others, when we invest in relationships, when we develop hearts of service, and when we promote peace. We know this!

Yet this is not what society likes to tell us. Society tells us we should chase the next, best job with a bigger salary, that our homes should look like a Pottery Barn catalog, and that our children should be tutored and talented, academic and athletic. Only then can we feel happiness, security, and true joy.

Friends, we know in our hearts this is ridiculous and yet we continue to fall for it. I know I do. I also know that striving for the outward trappings of success is meaningless work. It's peacocking. And it certainly doesn't create the deep, significant life change our Father wants for us. He didn't create us so we could amass wealth and possessions for our own satisfaction. We are blessed to be a blessing.

Many years ago, I sat with a seventy-year-old man named Bill. Bill's eyes crinkled when he smiled, revealing decades of good humor, kindness, and wisdom. Bill was a man filled with stories of people and places far beyond the

The Tools of the Trade

scope of what most of us have encountered. His life was rich with experiences, and he regaled me with countless stories about his lifelong service to God's mission.

While in their early thirties, Bill and his wife lived in a very remote island in the South Pacific. They were there to serve and give of themselves so others would come to know Jesus.

One day on the island, a man came to Bill's door and asked if he could borrow Bill's saw. The man was doing some work on his house and needed to cut some new pieces of wood. Bill quite happily loaned the man his saw. After a few days, the saw had not yet been returned. Bill wasn't sure how to approach the subject, and certainly didn't want to ruffle any islander feathers, so he waited. A week or so passed, and Bill finally encountered the man on the street. He said hello, and asked about the man's wife and children, his work, and his home, all the while hoping the man would mention the saw. But he didn't. No such luck. Bill decided not to bring it up either and instead chose to continue waiting.

Well, he waited and waited and waited. Many months later, Bill needed to use the saw himself, so he asked the man if he could have it back. The man directed Bill to another man who had borrowed the saw. When Bill approached that man, he was told to talk to another man who had also borrowed the saw. Bill followed the trail from one home to the next, to the next, to the next, and discovered that over the last few months—when the saw would have otherwise been sitting unused at Bill's home—it had been put to good use by six or seven different families. Sure enough, at the last home he found the saw and was able to complete his own improvement project.

LOVE CHILD

Bill smiled as he reflected on the way the islanders viewed community and resources. People did not look upon Bill's saw as "his" saw, it was "the" saw. The islanders viewed things as owned by the community as a whole, and they took responsibility for keeping things in good shape, knowing that if they accidentally broke something or neglected to care for it, it would impact the entire community's ability to use it.

That's a hard concept for those of us in the developed world to contemplate, isn't it? I mean, sure, I would lend my shovel to a neighbor. But if he went ahead and loaned my shovel to a complete stranger without asking me first, I'd probably be pretty annoyed. That's not very polite.

Bill's story makes me think I need to change my perspective on that. Or on a larger scale, maybe as Christians we should all be working to shift our collective viewpoint on possessions, for the benefit of God's kingdom.

How do you think God views my shovel? Is it mine, or is it a tool that should be shared freely—even beyond the scope of my "permission"?

What about something bigger, like my car? If I work from home, and a single mom in my community needs transportation to get to and from work a few days a week, do you think God would see my Subaru as "the" car?

What about something even bigger, like my finances? Do the immediate, sometimes urgent needs of others have to fit within the "giving" column of a budgeting spreadsheet? Or do I release my grip on my bank account, sharing my resources freely to help and bless others even when it may not make sense on paper?

Knowing God's heart for his children, and his desire that we would all take part in his mission, makes these questions easy to answer, yet so very hard to do. If you grew up in the church, you probably frequently heard the message that your finances were blessings from God, and all money is his, not ours. He is the owner of everything—everything I have is his. He is the Creator of all things, the Giver of all things. That message does a good job of setting the table for the mindset required to start breaking down the fence and blurring the property line between what's "ours" and what isn't. We're not giving what's ours, we're managing what's his. But actually putting it into practice can be a daily battle until you see the ways God steps in, often miraculously, to help us along the way.

A while back, I called the bank to see if I could refinance my mortgage. I had been watching rates drop and thought it might be a smart way to get a better interest rate and save some money each month. After explaining to the loan officer that I was interested in refinancing, she ran the math for me. "Actually, Mr. Peters," the woman said, "I'm not sure how you are affording your home right now. According to my calculations, you shouldn't have qualified for your current loan. I'm afraid we can't help you with refinancing."

To be honest, I didn't realize my financial picture was such that I wouldn't qualify for a refi. In all the years I've owned my home, I have never missed a mortgage payment. Still, according to the bank, I shouldn't be able to live here.

This relatively short conversation powerfully underscored my faith in God's provision. While yes, I live a simple, maybe even minimalistic lifestyle, it is abundantly clear that he provides.

LOVE CHILD

Countless times throughout my childhood, my mom and I stood in line at the soup kitchen and the food pantry. Being hungry and not knowing where you next meal is coming from is a scary existence—for adults and for children. Of course, food insecurity is often just one link in the chain that binds the poor. Consistent shelter is another. At one point when I was in high school, my mom and I were in a really hard place and struggling to pay rent. I distinctly remember the "thud" of an envelope that was pushed through our apartment door's mail slot, landing on our floor. We carefully opened the seal to discover $800 in cash—the exact amount we were short in rent that month!

I've been the recipient of people stewarding God's gifts as an expression of his love throughout all my life and in many different ways. It is my joy now to participate in that. Even when there's more month than money, the importance of generosity is not lost on me. It's not lost on Jesus, either.

> Jesus sat down opposite the place where the offerings were put and watched the crowd putting their money into the temple treasury. Many rich people threw in large amounts. But a poor widow came and put in two very small copper coins, worth only a few cents.
>
> Calling his disciples to him, Jesus said, "Truly I tell you, this poor widow has put more into the treasury than all the others. They all gave out of their wealth; but she, out of her poverty, put in everything—all she had to live on." (Mark 12:41–44)

When I was younger and just starting to exercise my generosity muscles, I used to buy Subway Sandwich gift cards and keep them in my wallet so I could give them to people who needed food. Over time, my giving

The Tools of the Trade

practices have changed, becoming more fluid. When I feel prompted, I give. Honestly, I don't even keep track anymore. I respond to opportunities when they arise. A ten-percent tithe is only a starting point. At the end of the day, everything we have belongs to God. Developing the faith in him to guide my generosity and loosen my grip on my finances has been significant and ongoing.

I don't think there's ever truly a finish line to this type of mindset shift when it comes to giving and generosity. We can always trust God a little more, respond to people's needs a little more quickly, and give a little (or maybe a lot) more. As children of God, there's always room for growth and improvement … along with a lot of grace. The prayer by Trappist monk and Catholic author, Thomas Merton—known as "The Merton Prayer"—is one my favorites, because it underscores the fact that this is a journey and we have a trail guide in God. Even if we don't always get our path or footwork right, our desire to follow him is what makes him happy. My favorite portion keeps it simple.

> My Lord God,
>
> I have no idea where I am going.
>
> I do not see the road ahead of me.
>
> I cannot know for certain where it will end.
>
> Nor do I really know myself,
>
> and the fact that I think that I am following your will
>
> does not mean that I am actually doing so.
>
> But I believe that the desire to please you
>
> does in fact please you.
>
> And I hope I have that desire in all that I am doing.

LOVE CHILD

Does your current walk reflect your goals? Are you in pursuit of people rather than possessions? Do you think you are headed in the right direction?

Years ago, a pastor was retiring from a long and productive career in ministry. As a farewell gift, he and his wife were given tickets to travel to Calcutta, India, so they could see firsthand the fruits of their labors. It was an amazing opportunity—one they could not wait to experience.

As it turns out, their daughter had just graduated from high school and was headed for college in the fall. The couple decided it might be the perfect opportunity to expand their daughter's view of the world by sharing this experience with her, so they scraped together the money and bought her a round-trip ticket to join them.

The three arrived in Calcutta and were picked up by a guide who took them to the place where Mother Teresa's ministry began. He ushered them into a small room with folding chairs and asked them to sit down. "I will go get someone to talk with you about this ministry," the guide said. The three sat there waiting, their eyes gazing around as they noted it was just four walls, a cement floor, and the ceiling. Aside from the folding chairs, there was no other furniture or décor in the room.

After a long while the door opened, and a tiny woman walked in. It was Mother Teresa. They were stunned. After decades of raising money and sending it to the ministry of this noble, faithful woman, here she was in living flesh, standing in front of them.

Mother Teresa slowly walked over to the three of them, pulling a folding chair along with her, and sat down directly in front of the young woman. She looked her

The Tools of the Trade

squarely in the eyes and said, "So tell me, what is it you are going to do with your life, my dear?"

Up to that point, the young high school graduate, Jennifer, had been asked by many people what her major was going to be, what she planned to study, and what type of career she wanted. But no one had ever asked her what she intended to do with her life.

Clearly, Mother Teresa knew this was the most important aspect of the family's visit. It wasn't about slapping the back of the father, thanking him for his ministry's prayers and support; it was about lighting a fire in the soul of the next generation, giving this young adult cause to reflect on what she wanted her own life to stand for, because there was still so much work to be done.

I think Mother Teresa's question that day has the power to completely alter our approach to life. Our hearts and hands are precious, and our time is limited. Do we want to spend our days amassing stuff that needs to be fixed, cleaned, and maintained? Or would that time and effort be better spent offering healing and hope to those who need it, in Jesus' name?

Let me be clear: possessions in and of themselves aren't bad. But if the bulk of our energy is spent in pursuit of more, I think we should try to do better. It's a daily choice, one we must make over and over again to break the cycle.

So how are you going to live your life? Do you want to pursue days marked by things that are temporal or experiences that are eternally significant?

11

The Original Marketer

When heaven is your audience, you live differently.
—Bobbie Houston

In the world of marketing, those who are most successful have developed an intimate understanding of who they are talking to—a group otherwise known as the target audience. These marketers know their target audiences' unmet needs and struggles, and they have the ability to pinpoint how they can ease their pain, bring them joy, or make life a little easier. Because they take the time to study these audience groups, they also figure out how to connect in a way that is relevant with the group's life stage and experience. In short, they are exceptionally good at customized interpersonal communication.

The marketer's golden rule of "know thy audience" was central to my career from the get-go: from my days presenting data to church leadership about how to better reach their neighbors and local communities, to my role at Compassion helping to shape the way key ministry opportunities were communicated to sponsors and donors.

You know who else knew this golden rule? Jesus. In fact, he was the originator of it. Jesus was an expert at crafting his message in a way that listeners could really receive it—I mean really let it sink in at a heart level.

LOVE CHILD

One of my favorite examples of this was when Jesus met the Samaritan woman at the well. On the surface, it's obvious: Jesus finds a woman at a well and shares about "living water." He builds a verbal bridge from where she is to where he wants to take her. But I've since learned it is so much deeper and more beautiful if we dip beneath the surface.

The pastor of my church, Pastor Glenn, shared this story in a way that made me rethink the narrative I have known and helped me see Jesus' love for this woman as even more incredible than I had previously thought.

If you attended church growing up, you've probably heard the story. You probably also were taught that this Samaritan was a dirty, sinful, promiscuous woman who made poor life choices (which was a thinly veiled way of saying she deserved her life circumstances). She had been married five times and was currently living with a man who was not her husband.

But to truly understand the power of this story, you need to look at it through the lens of the first century. That's critical, in fact, because it changes everything. The context here really matters, and it's a massive factor in understanding just how well Jesus "knew" his audience.

John 4 begins with Jesus and his disciples leaving Judea and heading north, by foot, to Galilee. In verse 6, John tells us that Jesus was sitting by Jacob's well because he was tired from the journey. It was about noon and the disciples had gone into town to buy food. A Samaritan woman came to the well, and Jesus asked her for a drink of water.

Seems simple enough, right? But there is so much more going on! Let's hit the pause button for a few first-century notes:

- **About Samaritans:** Jews traveling between Galilee and Judea would often voluntarily take a longer journey—crossing the Jordan River and traveling on the east side—rather than the shorter, direct route through Samaria. They avoided Samaria and Samaritans at all costs, believing they were an ignorant, impure race. But not Jesus. He chose to go through Samaria. This was on purpose. No matter what others thought about Samaritans, Jesus knew these people were his Father's children.

- **About the time of day:** People didn't collect water at noon because it was too hot. They went in the morning. In fact, women normally all went together in the morning so they could talk freely about their lives and families. This woman went at noon because she didn't want to be seen, and she most likely wasn't welcome to join the other women.

- **About women:** Women were viewed as property and as inferior to men in all matters. A woman could not divorce her husband. But a man could divorce his wife. This meant the Samaritan woman actually had no choice—and no voice—in her many marriages and divorces.

As Pastor Glenn framed it, for Jesus to initiate a conversation with a woman from this low-life, outcast, rejected, half-breed race was scandalous. Yet he did. And he didn't demand water from her, as a man typically would at this time and place. Jesus asked, "Will you give me a drink?" His question dignified and elevated her.

Her response was one of shock, as she questioned why he, a Jew, was even talking to her, a Samaritan.

They went on to talk about water, which was, of course, her reason for being at the well after all. Jesus made a very clear, compelling claim:

> Everyone who drinks this water will be thirsty again, but whoever drinks the water I give them will never thirst. Indeed, the water I give them will become in them a spring of water welling up to eternal life. (John 4:13–14)

As they talked, Jesus acknowledged the men in her past and affirmed that they could not fill her void. He introduced her to "living water"; to water that wouldn't leave her thirsty again and again; to water that would create a spring that would well up inside of her; to water that would provide the wholeness and fullness that he knew she had been desperately searching for over so many relationships and so many years. Jesus invited her to change her story, right then and there.

To quote Pastor Glenn,

> This is the story of a person from the lowest status of the most hated race in the worst town going through the hardest time of her life. And Jesus came to her. He restored her dignity by speaking with her about her life, without shame. He took time for her, investing in her present and eternal well-being by framing his message in a way she could understand, using water as the metaphor.

At the end of their conversation, the woman said, "I know that Messiah is coming. When he comes, he will explain everything to us." Jesus responded by saying, "I, the one speaking to you—I am he" (John 4:25–26).

Now if we want to go a bit deeper, we can look at the timing of this interaction in the life of Christ. When we do that, we realize that Jesus revealed his divinity to this low-life, outcast, rejected woman from a half-breed race *before* he affirmed Peter's bold confession that he is the Messiah. And as a result of this conversation—the longest conversation Jesus had with any woman in the four Gospels—she became an instant evangelist for Christ. Her destiny was forever changed.

This is a story about Christ's perfect brilliance and love.

- He contextualized his message to make it most relevant for this woman, at this time. He knew how to connect with her in a way that made sense.
- His wellspring of empathy and compassion opened up her heart.
  He cared about her past, and didn't judge her for it, inviting her instead to a new life.

This is also a story about a person who desperately craved real love and finally received it. This is the Jesus we follow. This is the Jesus who comes and seeks us. This is the love that we repeat and share with others who haven't heard and who desperately need to know that type of love, which only comes from Christ.

I want this to be the type of love that pours out of us in our day-to-day living. It is Christ's love through us, powered by the Holy Spirit, that can change the destiny of those who haven't heard, of those who don't know their value, and of those who have yet to drink from that spring and experience living water in a way that refreshes them each day.

Christ's love has the power to transform—and in the case of Gelil, to literally save lives.

LOVE CHILD

Gelil grew up in a Muslim family, in a Muslim community, in the Middle East. He saw God as the punisher and the controller. If Gelil didn't obey God's laws, he felt certain that he would be sent to hell. As Gelil grew up, his life was hard and he suffered from extreme loneliness. His mother was chronically ill, his dad didn't have a job, and they were very, very poor. When Gelil was a young adult, he joined the army, yet the loneliness he felt as a child wouldn't go away. He was depressed and struggled with fear, and he felt taunted by a voice inside his head telling him to kill himself.

While on holiday leave from the army, Gelil bumped into a friend.

This friend said he had become a Christian and he proceeded to talk about Jesus. When Gelil heard about this Messiah he had never known, he felt a warmth and power come over him that he couldn't explain. He began reading the Bible, and he was filled with a sense of love and peace that he had never experienced before.

Gelil finished his service with the army and went back to his village.

He continued reading the Bible and felt an urgency to share the good news with others. But he was in a Muslim society in which he could not worship in public. In fact, if the government found out, he could be jailed or killed.

Gelil heard that a Christian organization was building the first-ever school in his village. He applied for a job and was hired to work at the school as a security guard. Through the people he met there, he was encouraged to share his faith boldly, without fear.

Today Gelil talks openly in Muslim communities about the gospel of Jesus Christ. He is grateful for his kind friend

The Original Marketer

who first introduced him to God's life-changing gift of hope, and he now has a passion to do the same for others.

According to other Christians living in Gelil's community, it is apparent that God is using him in a very powerful way. He is a man of faith and fearlessness, growing the family of Christ through love and discipleship. He is no longer alone.

When we are able to step back and see the way God's hand has been at work in our lives, even through our darkest days, it can bring us to our knees. After so many years of feeling hopeless and lost myself, and questioning my identity, my value, and my reason for being, glimmers of light began to cut through the black, perhaps like the experiences of the Samaritan woman at the well and Gelil.

My turning point began with a trip to Panama.

12

How Then Shall We Live?

There is no heavier burden than an unfulfilled potential.
—**Charles Schulz**, creator of *Peanuts*

My spiritual retreat in the UK was monastic and contemplative, a pilgrimage toward a life that would be more vulnerable and available to God. It was part of a larger movement of believers, with people who were open, thoughtful, and comfortable with the reality that we live with more questions than answers. This refreshed my soul, as I had been plagued by the need to identify why my life had strayed so far from my intended path.

Removing myself from the noise of my life at home gave me the peace and space to be fully present with God and rediscover his grace. I learned to keep company with him and listen to him with ears unburdened by negative self-talk. It was at this retreat that I could finally, blissfully rest. As Thomas Merton once said, "Where you are is where you belong." Acknowledging and honestly assessing the current state of my life at that time, without the peripheral buzz of opinions and condemnation by others, gave me the opportunity to accept where I was and put a stake in the ground, claiming a defining moment in how my next chapters would unfold. It was clear I needed Jesus to lead the way, and I was more than ready to let him do so.

LOVE CHILD

Shortly after returning home, I was hired by a Christian publisher and music label to oversee sales and partnership opportunities outside of the English-speaking world. One of our clients was holding an international leadership meeting in Panama, and I was invited to attend as a representative of the publishing house. The client was Operation Mobilisation (OM), a global community of Jesus followers who have a passion to live and share the gospel with others to the farthest corners of the world.

At the conference, I experienced a next-level awakening. I was surrounded by people who were actively loving and caring for others all over the world. These were folks who thought that when Jesus said "Go into all the world" and "Love your neighbor" he really meant it. Their normalness was refreshing. They weren't supermodels with disarmingly white teeth and Instagram-influencer magnetism. They weren't self-proclaimed Christian superheroes either, wielding their Bibles with pomp and authority. They were beautifully ordinary people choosing to live extraordinary lives for God. Their spirits were humble, their love for God's creation was real, and their desire to play an active role in his mission here on earth was sincere. I fell hard for their ministry.

I made my heart's desire known to God, a hope that I would have the opportunity to someday join this group of life evangelists at OM. Later I received a phone call from an OM leader who wanted to chat about marketing, and in a matter of months I joined the OM team as chief marketing officer.

As you read this, you may think this all happened rather fast. And in hindsight, I suppose it did. But while I waited and wondered if my prayers would be answered, it all felt rather slow. And in the grand scheme of my recent years, it seemed like it was a long time coming.

How Then Shall We Live?

As I embraced the scope of my new job at OM, I decided it would be wise to understand our audience better. I needed to understand the connection between Christians and God's work in the world today. At first glance, the data I found raised a number of red flags. There are approximately 2.5 billion people in the world who profess to be Christians,[6] yet only 435,000 people (less than one-tenth of 1 percent) engage in cross-cultural missions. And Christians today, on average, give 2.5 percent of their income to churches.[7]

If Christianity was not inherently designed for sharing, these statistics might be understandable. But serving, loving, and taking delight in delivering Christ's teachings to others is central to who we are. Actively engaging in God's mission is the essence of how we should be living each and every day.

No, these data points were not just disappointing—they were alarming; and they opened the floodgates to a rush of questions. Do Christians understand God's call to global mission? How can we communicate with them more effectively so that they understand their role in the kingdom? What types of messages or approaches would resonate best?

I couldn't find what I was looking for using traditional resources. The numbers were clear: to inspire Christians for God's mission, I knew we needed to better understand their hearts and perspectives. I also recognized that the global landscape of Christianity is vibrant and textured, with distinct variances among countries, cultures, and communities. So I decided to launch an original-research initiative by commissioning top consumer-research and data-analysis firms in seven different countries to design and moderate focus-group discussions that were in keeping with the native language and culture.

The findings were fascinating—and depressing. Christians across all countries possessed a high level of awareness about their role in sharing the love of Christ with others. So we delved into another layer of questioning. What do they believe their role on earth *is*? What stops them from taking part in God's mission in a bigger way? What are the visible and invisible hurdles preventing them from taking action? Are they content with how they live out faith in their daily lives? Are they somehow ashamed of their faith? Through hypotheticals, the moderators worked to uncover what was preventing people from actively sharing the gospel. By the end of every focus group—regardless of the country, or the age of participants, or the language—people had excuse after excuse after excuse as to why they didn't take action.

I learned that the majority of Christians don't know that being a Christian means participating in a movement focused on God's work in the world. Most of us think it is just about living a good life, being nice to others, teaching our kids right from wrong, and sometimes recycling.

In other words, the study revealed that the majority of Christians understand that we are to love God and love others. But very few know that this is only part of the story. We don't realize we are called to bring his love to the corners of the world.

We understand the Great Commandment, but not the Great Commission.

> All authority in heaven and on earth has been given to me. Therefore go and make disciples of all

nations, baptizing them in the name of the Father and of the Son and of the Holy Spirit, and teaching them to obey everything I have commanded you. And surely I am with you always, to the very end of the age. (Matt 28:18–20)

This passage is most commonly known as the Great Commission, and according to a 2018 report by Barna, 51 percent of US churchgoers say they have not heard of it.[8] This aligned with my own findings. And not just in the US, but in Australia, Brazil, Chile, Germany, Ghana, and Hong Kong as well.

The bottom line is that work clearly needs to be done within the church to help people understand the exciting mission God has cast before them—locally and globally.

As believers, all of us have joined a movement, been given tools and skills to contribute to that movement and have been told the goal. So why don't most Christians know this? And what about the rest of us, who understand the Great Commission but don't act on it? What's going on with us?

The focus groups around the world revealed that fear keeps us from action. There are a variety of sources of fear, which we'll get into in the next few chapters, but the common thread throughout is that we're not sure God will show up to help us engage in the role he has called us to play, so we don't even pick up the script.

13

Fruitless

Courage isn't just a matter of not being frightened, you know. It's being afraid and doing what you have to do anyway.

—Doctor Who

Moses is one of my favorite characters in the Bible because he's such a relatable guy. He struggled with self-doubt, felt ill-equipped for the work ahead of him, and experienced a real, sweat-inducing fear of failure.

In Exodus 3–4, God spoke to Moses from within a burning bush to deliver a massive job description: "I am sending you to Pharaoh to bring my people the Israelites out of Egypt" (Exod 3:10).

This was an overwhelming assignment for Moses. He would have to confront the pharaoh, the most powerful political figure in the region, to demand the release of hundreds of thousands of Israelites, ending a long and well-established tradition of slavery. He reacted as I think many of us would, saying with disbelief, "Who? Me?" while looking nervously over his shoulder.

As God reassured Moses, he started lobbing out every excuse he could think of. "What if they don't believe you sent me?" "But I'm not eloquent enough!" And finally, out of sheer fear, he begged God, "Please send someone else!"

LOVE CHILD

Moses was scared out of his mind! I think we all would have been if we were in his shoes. But what Moses eventually learned—a lesson each and every one of us today needs to learn—is that the fate of the world was not on his shoulders. This was God's mission and God's assignment, and God's strength and provision was going to get him through. His job was not to be adequate enough for the task. His job was to show up, push his fears aside, and do what he was told.

As Moses began to take steps forward and actually follow God's directions, he began to see that God was walking with him at every turn. God was not going to abandon him; he was equipping Moses with the right words, at the right time. Moses began to see that the only way he was going to achieve this massive mission was through God's grace. Of course, he came across obstacles and made mistakes; but God was always there, providing exactly what Moses needed so that the mission could continue and Moses could successfully lead the slaves out of Egypt.

This story is one I love because it should serve as a source of relief to us all. It's not about us! It's not about our self-assessed skill level, or capacity, or eloquence, or charm. God only knows what we are capable of achieving for the kingdom.

This is about our choice to act.

When we do what we can do, God will do what only he can do. When Moses channeled his fear into faith, he became a massive force for God's mission in the world.

Moses' apprehension was rooted in a fear of failure, which was one of the three types of fear the "mission gap" research revealed as a massive barrier for Christians worldwide. It's a self-protective type of fear: "What if I give my life for a cause and it's a failure? I don't want to fail!"

Fruitless

Of course, no one wants to be a failure or to be associated with a fruitless endeavor. For those of us raised in an environment or culture that demands proof of effectiveness, actively rewards achievement, and measures return-on-investment, our fear of failure is hard-wired. It tells us that we'd better not jump into something unless we're positive that it's going to make a difference—assuming, of course, that we're the ones who get to decide whether or not a difference was made.

For people who are raised in an environment around scarcity, where there's a limited or finite amount of resources to go around, fear of failure can be rooted in a desire to appropriate resources judiciously … carefully … responsibly. We want to check and double-check every last detail to make sure we are implementing the most efficient plan possible.

At a psychological level, I think one could argue that a fear of failure may indicate a higher level of conscientiousness rooted in an earnest desire to do well and an understanding of the stakes—all good stuff! However, regardless of the reasoning behind it, what trips us up is not the fear itself but the inaction that it causes.

Allowing fear to be the roadblock that prevents us from acting is where we all go awry. Akin to our Moses story, it's not our job to project outcomes or to predict winners and losers. Our job is to suit up and play the game. I truly believe with all my heart that God is more interested in our willingness to follow his commands than he is in the result of the work.

One Christ follower in Ashland, Virginia, knew this. I've personally never met him, but I've witnessed the impact of his service in Jesus's name.

LOVE CHILD

Several years ago, I was traveling in India while working with Compassion International. Our team flew into Mumbai and then drove for a full day to reach a small church in a remote little village. We were there to talk about the safe-water project we had been working on with the church. We sat down to talk with the pastor, and he informed us the bishop would be joining us.

We chatted for a while, and soon the bishop arrived. After asking about his life and family, I inquired why he was called the bishop when the church was not part of any larger denomination. He said they call him the bishop because he planted that particular church and was part of a team that planted two hundred other churches in India.

I was intrigued and wanted to know more about his childhood and spiritual life.

He said he was raised by a single mother who was severely disabled. Her mobility was very limited, and as a result she had a hard life. One day, his mother heard that Jesus was a couple of villages away, healing people. Something in his mother's spirit clicked into gear. She collected her walking sticks and slowly made her way onto a bus and over to the village to see Jesus.

Of course, it wasn't actually Jesus who was there. It was a man from the United States who was talking about Jesus.

That day, his mother heard the gospel message for the first time and was completely overcome with emotion. She edged her way to the front of the crowd and received a healing. Later she returned home to her village, without any need for her walking sticks and with a Bible under her arm. She was truly healed. She couldn't read the Bible, but her son, the man who would one day be called the bishop, could read it. He read it to her every night for years, and over time he came to faith in Christ himself. It was at that point that he joined the church-planting team.

When the bishop reflects on all of the people who have come to faith because of that first interaction between his mother and God in that remote village, through the faithfulness of a Christ follower from the US, the bishop says he is filled with gratitude. "If I get to Virginia one day, I'm going to find that church and thank them," he said. "Now we have hundreds of churches in India all because of what God did through that one person."

The man from Virginia may not be aware of the light that is spreading in India thanks to his courage. He may have left wondering if anything ever happened as a result of his work. But that's OK. God measures failure and success in his time, not ours. This man did what he was told, and that's really all that matters.

So here's the question: Are we willing to stop using human, worldly tools to measure our effectiveness? Are we OK with making investments that we may never know the results of on this side of heaven? Are we comfortable not having a success story to share with friends and family around the Thanksgiving table or a neat and tidy impact statement for our resume? Being wise and diligent when making a decision is one thing; attempting to measure the real impact God wants to have is quite another.

The thing about fear is that at the end of the day, just being afraid doesn't mean our assignment goes away. Or that our Commander will no longer call on us. Me being afraid, you being afraid, does not change God's direction. It's really just about what we're willing to go through to follow him. What will you push through?

LOVE CHILD

How are you going to let faith, instead of fear, guide your days?

It's not an easy path, but once you begin to build the right muscles, it is so incredibly freeing! It's like going to the gym regularly. For those of us who want to keep pursuing spiritual growth, we've gotta show up and do the work. Of course, some days will be much harder than others.

14

Chris-Cross

The gray area, the place between black and white—that's the place where life happens.
—**Justin Timberlake**

During a brief moment of clarity while I was unemployed, suddenly single, and generally reeling from my life circumstances, God's voice sliced through the chaos within my mind. In a moment, I knew I had to get back out and be with people. I started at a bar.

It was a local, hole-in-the-wall kind of place. It was small and comforting and safe; it was a place where I could simply have a beer and be part of a community of people who had their own layered stories. Plus, it had great music, a chatty but chill bartender, good beer, and was within walking distance of my house. I've since learned that it is one of a few local establishments frequented by the local gay community.

One night a guy and I started talking. He introduced himself as Christopher and it looked like he and the woman next to him were together. We chatted for about twenty minutes, covering sports and a mix of random topics. Then we came to the inevitable part of the conversation: the "What do you do?" part.

"Well," I said. "I've spent my entire life in missions and ministry. I've served as a pastor and also with a number of Christian nonprofits."

And just like that, everything changed. Christopher went from lively and chatty to quiet and disengaged. Since I really had nothing to lose, I decided to find out what was going on.

"Huh, as soon as I mention the church, you're done?" I inquired. "I'm guessing you've got some thoughts or feelings on the subject."

Christopher leaned back on his stool so I could fully see the woman sitting next to him. "This is my wife," he said. "We're getting divorced because I'm gay, so the church and I are at odds these days. I'm basically sinning twice—I'm gay and getting a divorce. In my experience, people of faith really have nothing to say to me."

I sincerely wanted to know the details of Christopher's story. Once he could tell I wasn't there to shame him, he opened up.

He shared the story of growing up in the church and being raised as a Roman Catholic child inside a very devout Roman Catholic family. He talked about being active in the church as an acolyte and even contemplating the idea of the priesthood for a while. But as he approached his early twenties, he began to distance himself from the church. He felt the teachings became very harsh and cold. They were centered on rules, and he just couldn't figure out how to live by the code.

When he met the woman who would become his wife, she was not Catholic. But knowing it was important to him, she took the steps to be baptized and officially became a Catholic before they wed. They were married in a Roman Catholic church.

Christopher said he remembered feeling from the beginning that something wasn't quite right. But if you're not going to become a priest, good Catholic men get married and have a family. That was his accepted path—his destiny. However, shortly after the birth of their daughter, Christopher gained more clarity around his feelings of unrest. He had begun to struggle with his sexuality.

Christopher jolted out of his reflectiveness and said, "Now, after twenty years of marriage, we are getting a divorce." Even though he knew divorce was a sin, Christopher had been raised with too much respect for the institution of marriage as ordained by God to remain in it and make a mockery of what God had designed. He felt trapped—damned if he stayed and damned if he left. Both options meant sin, and in his eyes the church would disregard him either way.

In Christopher's eyes, after a lifetime of commitment to the church, the church offered judgment and damnation in return—and not just once, but twice. The only thing he knew to be true of the church at this point in his life was that he was no longer welcome.

Christopher and I talked for quite a while about his life, the church, and the pain of realizing that in perhaps the most difficult season of his life, the very foundation of faith and Catholic community that were established beneath him as a child were being pulled out from under him. As he was losing his marriage and family, he was also losing his church.

I couldn't help but see correlations to my own story. I, too, had grown up in the church. I, too, had felt the scorn and rebuke of Christians after my divorce. And I, too, was hurt in part because the church had completely missed the concepts of grace, forgiveness, and love.

LOVE CHILD

As Christians, it's clear that most of us have failed to see the larger picture of what God's mission on earth is all about: finding those who don't know his love, and sharing it openly and generously with everyone, as Jesus would.

The very nature of Christ and the church is wrapped in his unrelenting love and his tireless pursuit of those who need it the most. Yet for whatever reason, we, his followers, often act as if we know nothing of the loving nature of the God we claim to follow. Or maybe we've just forgotten.

Christopher asked for my number to see if we could talk again, and we met up for coffee two weeks later. He shared more about his life, and I shared with him that God's love is at the core of everything the church stands for. I apologized that he had been given a cold, judgmental picture of God.

I still see him around town. Sometimes I see him with his ex-wife and daughter. In the midst of his heartbreak about the church, he was also heartbroken about what the divorce might mean for his teenage daughter, so he and his wife have agreed to co-parent as best they can, remaining an active, united part of her life.

Following a faith built on rules alone is impossible. The Pharisees throughout history, both ancient and those still plotting today, are full of rules for how to live the best Christian life. Yet one thing I know to be true is that rules will kill the love God wants us to nurture and set free throughout the world in his name.

While serving in the Middle East, a friend of mine was presented with an impossible challenge of Christian teaching and outreach. For some time, he had been sharing about his Christian faith with his Muslim neighbor. The man had three wives, as was the custom in that part of the world. When this man decided to come to faith in Christ, he asked my friend, "I read that man is supposed to have only one wife. How do I decide which of my wives to divorce?"

After giving this problem a great deal of thought, my friend replied, "I'm certain that if you ask five different Christians you could receive five different answers to this question. When faced with impossible decisions, or biblical teachings that appear to be contradictory, I tend to seek the answer that is the most loving. Love has to be the foundation, not the rules."

He went on to advise the man that as far as he could tell, the most loving thing to do was to keep all three wives and take no more. In that culture, a divorced woman would have been left to fend for herself for the rest of her life. She would have been mistreated, shunned, and viewed as an outcast.

It's ironic to me that the rules and commandments God originally gave us to help us draw closer to him are so often used instead to point a judgmental finger and divide his children from one another. What's that about a speck in our brother's eye and a plank of wood in our own?

I think that if sharing the gospel with someone involves demeaning or belittling them, you're doing it wrong. If talking about our faith with someone who doesn't know Christ makes it seem as if we're better than they are, we've missed the point of transformation. We're not better, we may just be in a different spot. Either way, we're on the same road.

Anyone who tells you that living a Christian life is black and white either hasn't faced a heart-wrenching situation or is cloaked in a protective layer of righteousness so thick that it's preventing them from seeing the world through Christ's eyes.

Thankfully, his love has the power to permeate the gray spaces.

15

White-Knuckle Grip

A comfort zone is a beautiful place, but nothing ever grows there.

—Unknown

I have a friend who is a quasi-vegetarian. She's a vegetarian who eats fish and, when the mood strikes, chicken. She's not working up to becoming a full-blown vegetarian. She's not pursuing this lifestyle because of her religion, or her concern for the environment, or her stance on animal rights. It's simply her personal brand of vegetarianism. If you would ask most people, they would probably tell you that she's not a vegetarian—she just doesn't eat red meat.

I think many of us view our Christianity like my friend views her vegetarianism. We label ourselves Christian and claim to follow Jesus, but then want to pick and choose when we live out our faith with others. We do it when it's convenient, or when we feel comfortable, or when we have the time, or when we have the financial buffer in place. We opt out when chicken parmesan is on the menu.

As Christians, we get to be part of the greatest mission of love and hope the world has ever seen. We have the privilege of using our unique talents and skills and training and wiring to accomplish the mission God has been on since the very beginning—to unify all of his children to their loving Father. This is not a part-time task. It's an all-in scenario.

LOVE CHILD

I've been listening to the music of Lindy & The Circuit Riders lately. In their song "Take Courage," there's a verse that grabs me:

> And I can feel the drum of Your heartbeat
>
> You're calling us to be Your hands and feet
>
> We're rising up with courage in our hearts
>
> To carry out Your love to the hardest and the dark

This is deeply compelling to me because our job, as Christians, is to bring Christ's love to others on earth. We aren't supposed to stay comfortable, in our brightly lit Christian church bubbles, nurturing our own faith walks. We were made to have eyes that look out, into the darkness, beyond our own needs and wants and desires. Of course, doing so requires sacrifice.

Jesus was very clear that we are to love our neighbors as ourselves. When asked to define what he meant by "neighbor," he could have given a simple answer, but instead Jesus told the parable of the Good Samaritan (Luke 10:30–37). It's a story you probably know well. While a Jewish man was walking on a road, he was severely beaten and left for dead by a group of robbers. Both a priest and a Levite came upon the man, and when they saw him they passed by on the other side of the road. But when the Samaritan saw the beaten man, he took pity on him.

Jesus elaborated on the lengths the Samaritan went to so he could love his neighbor:

> He went to him and bandaged his wounds, pouring on oil and wine. Then he put the man on his own donkey, brought him to an inn and took care of him. The next day he took out two denarii and gave

White-Knuckle Grip

them to the innkeeper. "Look after him," he said, "and when I return, I will reimburse you for any extra expense you may have." (Luke 10:34–35)

Not only is this a story of extraordinary cross-cultural care, it's made even more powerful because we know that, at the time, Jews and Samaritans hated each other.

Would you go into debt to take care of an enemy? Would I?

What about a more typical scenario today? If you walked by a homeless man on the street who needed food, would you buy him lunch? Or keep walking? What if you saw someone at the park who seemed confused and might need medical attention? Would you drive her to the emergency room and sit with her in the waiting room? What if a neighbor's home was destroyed by a tornado or hurricane? Would you invite that family to stay in your home?

Man, these are tough questions for me. If you're really giving them honest consideration, they're probably challenging you too. They're difficult because I think we truly *want* to help others. But so often, the busyness of our lives gets in the way. I am 100-percent sure that if I had room in my schedule, I would sit with the stranger in the emergency room. If my basement wasn't occupied by a renter, I would take in the family who needed shelter. And if I wasn't already fifteen minutes late for my doctor's appointment, I would go to the nearest restaurant and buy the homeless man lunch. That represents a lot of good intentions and a lot of ifs, but no guarantee of action.

Maybe we all need to make more space in our lives for God's mission.

I read a book about a long-distance runner who blocked off entire days to run, with no particular route in mind. He'd grab $20 and a bottle of water and just go. He was never sure what the day would bring, but he was open to wherever the road took him.

I remember reading that and thinking we Christians should approach life that way. We should regularly set aside time—even full days—where we walk out our front door with a little cash and a prayer that God would use us as he sees fit, guiding us to cross paths with people in need of his love and care.

Of course, doing this would likely require some type of sacrifice—that is, unless you are living on a trust fund with no one to care for other than yourself! But for the rest of us, it might mean giving up a free Saturday afternoon so that instead of watching basketball on the couch or going shopping with friends, we could volunteer at a soup kitchen or homeless shelter. Or maybe it means we forego our lunch hour once a week to drive around the city streets and hand out care packages with food, socks, body wipes, and deodorant. There are a lot of small ways we can start loving our neighbors, but first we have to loosen our grip on our own personal comfort.

We need to remember, however, that the concept of sacrifice is foreign to society today. Some of the loudest messages across network television, social media, and podcasts encourage us to put ourselves first. "Do what makes you happy" and "focus on self-care" are not just expressions, they're a way of life preached by people who believe that only by caring for and embracing yourself can you "live your best life." It's all about pursuing the career that you want, getting the salary you deserve, designing your life around *your* truth. It's secular heaven and it encourages self-worship.

White-Knuckle Grip

For those who don't have a relationship with Jesus, this makes sense. They have no reason to put the interests of anyone else above themselves. But for Christians, living a me-centered life means we've pushed God off his throne and put ourselves there in his place.

A lot of us have also wrapped our brains around this idea that we are the providers. But that's a false God too. The core reality of the Christian faith is that God is our provider. He provides everything we need. He created everything, owns everything, and gives everything.

God did not provide us with all that we have so that we can buy a bigger house, pay for a better vacation, or have fewer wrinkles. He provided us with what we have so that we can choose to use it for his mission to love others in the world.

> Do not forget to do good and to share with others, for with such sacrifices God is pleased. (Heb 13:16)

I know that completely handing over our lives to God is a very uncomfortable thing for people to think about. In the research studies, it was crystal clear that people have a fear of sacrifice when it comes to jumping into the Great Commission. They're afraid of what it might mean for their family to sell their house, uproot from their neighborhood schools, and travel to a part of the world with few churches and fewer Christians—if any at all.

Of course, this doesn't mean all Christians need to travel overseas to share the love of Jesus with others. But we do need to develop eyes that see, hearts that are filled with compassion, and hands and feet that take action, bringing healing and relief to those who need it.

I remember hearing a knock at the door when I was about five years old. Three people from church dropped by unexpectedly. It was December, and they were carrying bags of groceries, a real Christmas tree, and wrapped gifts.

One of the gifts for me was a stuffed animal that could stand up on two feet, like a human. It was a dog wearing a brown jacket and a yellow scarf. I named him Joey and slept with him for the next few years.

Loving your neighbor can start small and local. It doesn't always involve plane tickets. But as followers of Christ, and servants of God's mission in the world, we should be receptive to the Master's direction. The heart of our Father breaks if people are hurting or suffering, or if they don't know their real value and haven't experienced God's true love. No matter where they are, we need to be ready to act.

My friend Seelan and I were talking over coffee one morning about this very topic—about how a Christian's heart should break for what breaks God's heart—and he shared a new perspective with me on the parable of the prodigal son in Luke 15:11–32.

> There was a man who had two sons. The younger one said to his father, "Father, give me my share of the estate." So he divided his property between them.
>
> Not long after that, the younger son got together all he had, set off for a distant country and there squandered his wealth in wild living. After he had spent everything, there was a severe famine in that whole country, and he began to be in need. So he went and hired himself out to a citizen of that country, who sent him to his fields to feed pigs. He longed to fill his stomach with the pods that the pigs were eating, but no one gave him anything.

White-Knuckle Grip

When he came to his senses, he said, "How many of my father's hired servants have food to spare, and here I am starving to death! I will set out and go back to my father and say to him: Father, I have sinned against heaven and against you. I am no longer worthy to be called your son; make me like one of your hired servants." So he got up and went to his father.

But while he was still a long way off, his father saw him and was filled with compassion for him; he ran to his son, threw his arms around him and kissed him.

The son said to him, "Father, I have sinned against heaven and against you. I am no longer worthy to be called your son."

But the father said to his servants, "Quick! Bring the best robe and put it on him. Put a ring on his finger and sandals on his feet. Bring the fattened calf and kill it. Let's have a feast and celebrate. For this son of mine was dead and is alive again; he was lost and is found." So they began to celebrate.

Meanwhile, the older son was in the field. When he came near the house, he heard music and dancing. So he called one of the servants and asked him what was going on. "Your brother has come," he replied, "and your father has killed the fattened calf because he has him back safe and sound."

The older brother became angry and refused to go in. So his father went out and pleaded with him. But he answered his father, "Look! All these years I've been slaving for you and never disobeyed your orders. Yet you never gave me even a young goat so I could celebrate with my friends. But when this son of yours who has squandered your property with prostitutes comes home, you kill the fattened calf for him!"

"My son," the father said, "you are always with me, and everything I have is yours. But we had to celebrate and be glad, because this brother of yours was dead and is alive again; he was lost and is found."

Seelan said that it amazes him how many Christians hear that story and automatically think of themselves as the son who moved away, led a rowdy life, and then came back only to be welcomed with open arms by his father. "Everyone wants to be the one whom the Father welcomes home," he said. "But in reality, I think most of us Christians are the other son. We know our brother is not at home, see the pain and anguish on our Father's face each day for his lost son, and do nothing about it."

Ouch!

But you know what? He's right. The brother knew his father was in pain, but did nothing about it. Worse yet, we read in the story that the brother who stayed seemed to know where his brother had gone and what he was up to. He knew, yet did nothing. Day after day, he could have gone to find his lost brother and bring him home, but he didn't. Instead, he was angry when his brother returned to the open arms of their father.

If we don't have hearts to seek out our lost brothers and sisters, then is the heart's cry of our heavenly Father really that important to us? And not just locally, but all over the world?

The best estimates report that there are three billion people in the world today who don't live near a church, have no Christian neighbors, and who will likely live their entire lives without ever knowing of God's deep love for them.[9] Yes, that's billion—with a "b." That three-billion number doesn't account for the non-Christian people who *do* live near Christian neighbors (like you and me). We just have to cross the street to show people in our community that they are loved. For the other three billion, we have to go a lot farther.

Time and time again we hear Jesus declare what to do if we love him: "Feed my sheep ... love your neighbor as yourself ... go into the world and make disciples." He couldn't be clearer. Have you ever stopped to consider the last words of Christ on earth before his ascension? They're recorded in Acts 1:8:

> You will receive power when the Holy Spirit comes on you; and you will be my witnesses in Jerusalem, and in all Judea and Samaria, and to the ends of the earth.

We have received our marching orders. If our hearts are aligned with God's heart, that should direct our actions in every way—from how we steward our finances to how we spend our time. God's heart tells us where to focus.

Christ didn't die for 10 percent of our paychecks and our worship at church on Sundays. It was for something much, much bigger.

He died so we would go all-in.

In fact, that's the whole reason God created us, that we might choose to serve him with our entire being. If we miss that, we miss the very point of our existence.

I know change is scary. The thought of sacrifice is too. It's a sacrifice to put your trust in God's provision instead of the things of the world. And yes, it means that you might not earn the income that you were earning before, or you might need to downsize your spending to support God's mission somewhere else in the world. Your children might end up being raised in an environment where your native language is really only spoken at home, or they will have to get used to a different way of living with different customs and different foods. But is that a sacrifice you're willing to make so that someone can see the living example of Christ's love in the world? So they can understand, maybe for the first time, that God loves them?

At its root, I think our fear of sacrifice is actually being afraid to trust God fully—in his purpose, his plans, and his provision for the journey ahead. Ironically, we have nothing to be afraid of losing, because it's not ours in the first place. That makes this an exercise in stewardship, not sacrifice. If our time, money, property, family, friends, job, and all our other "assets" are God's, and he has entrusted them to us, then it's not a question of whether we will sacrifice it all, but rather a question of how we will channel what we have to accomplish his work in the world.

I have to make clear that I haven't got this nailed down in my own life. I still put my trust in things. And I still get distracted by things that have zero impact on God's mission. But my desire every day is to have a trajectory that leads toward wrapping my entire life around God's mission.

There is a worship song by Hillsong titled "So Will I" that ends with the following:

If You gladly chose surrender so will I

I can see Your heart

Eight billion different ways

Every precious one

A child You died to save

If You gave Your life to love them so will I.[10]

The "eight billion" in the song refers to the population

of the world: all people, all faiths, all races, the whole crazy mix. God's heart breaks because there are people in the world—his children—who don't know him or his love, and he has asked for our help in reuniting the family. If that's what a Christian is, then that's what I want to do. That's what I want to make my life about. That's what Bill is doing.

Bill is a physician I know. He had an incredibly successful practice in the United States but moved to serve as a doctor in the Middle East, where they need doctors and Christians are few and far between. Bill does not have a Messiah complex. His decision to move to the Middle East was actually pretty simple. He looked at what God had given him and asked a question: Since I'm called to share the gospel with my full life, and I have my current education, experience, passion, and training to offer, how do I build a bridge to make it happen in a place that would make the biggest difference? How do I take what God has given me and go and do the thing he has commanded me?

And so Bill now works at a hospital in the Middle East, where many people have not encountered Christians before. He regularly has conversations with people who are amazed at his bedside manner, at the way he seems to really care for his patients, and his commitment to go the extra mile. Hospital administrators, fellow doctors, nurses, and others regularly come to Bill and ask why he seems to have such a different attitude. Is it part of the training he received in the United States? Is it from taking some sort of special class in doctor/patient bedside manner? He just says, "No, it's because I'm a follower of Jesus. I've seen the way God loves me, and I want to treat others the same way."

LOVE CHILD

Bill didn't move to the Middle East to prove anything. He moved because he was following God's call and using the tools and equipment God gave him. And yes, it was and is a sacrifice. He sacrificed the career track he was on, being close to family and friends he has known all his life, and countless creature comforts he may have otherwise taken for granted in the United States.

Bill's story is also a reminder that stepping into God's mission with our entire lives will require an acceptance of change, but we don't need to step outside of who we are. For example, you don't need to be a church planter if you don't have the skills, training, or passion for that. You don't need to go door-to-door sharing the gospel if you are really introverted and prefer longer lasting, one-on-one relationships. We just need to use what God has given us.

16

Chocolate or Vanilla

*What really matters is what you do
with what you have.*
—**H. G. Wells**, *Soul of a Bishop*

It has always been very important to me to have a close relationship with my son. Surely this is due in part to the absence of my own father as I was growing up. Contrary to my childhood, I wanted to be there for my son, not just for his milestones but also for the more mundane, everyday things like making him chocolate chip pancakes, driving him to school, and taking him shopping for pants.

When Mason was about seven years old we started going on road trips together. He would pick the destination, we'd hop in the car, and we'd go. Our first father-son road trip was a long weekend to South Dakota to see Mount Rushmore. I'm sure Mason appreciated the grand scale and majesty of America's founding fathers in granite, but I think his highlights from that inaugural trip were rooted in our collective abandonment of bedtime so we could watch movies, order pizza, and—when we finally woke up in the morning—revisit the pizza box for breakfast. It was a classic guy weekend, and a memory I still treasure.

Ever since that first trip, we've built on this little tradition of ours. To date, Mason and I have been to forty-two states together. The goal of each trip has been to see something Mason was interested in. Not a city or town, but a landmark of sorts. When he was nine he wanted to see the Seattle Space Needle, so we packed our tent and sleeping bags and took off.

During this time, Mason was really into origami. He had read a book about it and was fascinated by the forms you could make with a simple piece of paper. His little fingers were quick and light as he transformed all shapes and colors of paper into birds, mammals, and figurines. His love for *Star Wars* intersected with his craft when he learned the ultimate table trick: how to make a green origami Yoda out of a dollar bill.

In Seattle we stopped at Ye Old Curiosity Shop, a place that was more museum than store. It was a treasure trove, jam-packed with curios, novelty items, carvings, mummified bodies, shrunken heads, and, as it turns out, origami figures made out of dollar bills. We had hit the motherlode. This store that was founded in 1899 transported us to another dimension. Mason was enthralled as we walked through the aisles, spotting tusks and fir-needle baskets, taking special note of the origami along the way. After making it through every square inch of Ye Old Curiosity Shop, Mason quietly noted it was without a Yoda figurine.

That evening, back at the hotel, he went to work, meticulously folding dollar bills until he had the perfect George Washington Yoda. The next day, we went back to the shop to inquire if they would be interested in putting it on display. As it turns out, they were. Mason was over the moon ... beyond any thrill the Space Needle had to offer. We still talk about going back to Seattle someday to see if Yoda lives on.

To you, these might seem like simple, maybe even unremarkable, father-son moments. And I guess they are.

But they're made all the more special to me when I think about Mason's start to life. It wasn't easy.

When Mason was about two years old, we took him to the pediatrician for a standard well-child checkup. We knew he had a speech delay, but we weren't overly concerned, thinking he would catch up. The doctor, however, gave us a benchmark, telling us that by the age of two a stranger should be able to understand 50 percent of everything Mason said. His mother and I were devastated as we realized his words were rarely intelligible to others.

As luck would have it, Mason's godmother was a speech pathologist. Contrary to the pediatrician's advice to "wait and see if he catches up," she urged us to get assistance right away to afford Mason the earliest intervention possible.

That's when Jill the speech therapist entered our lives, coming to our house multiple times each week for therapy sessions with Mason. We bought baskets full of learning tools and aids and started implementing activities into our daily routine to encourage Mason's language development. We hoped Jill's one-on-one work with Mason and our painfully intentional efforts around the house would yield results. And they did. But Mason's improvement did not pace with Jill's expectations. She suggested Mason be tested to see if he was on the autism spectrum.

Autism?

Honestly, it was a six-letter throat punch.

In quick succession, I felt all of the stereotypes land with unbearable, heavy thuds upon my shoulders. Would Mason be able to speak in full sentences? Get a job? Be independent? Would my son be like Rain Man?

We took Mason to see Dr. Pauline Filipek, one of the leading researchers on autism spectrum disorders at that time in Orange County, California, where we lived. After a developmental screening process and diagnostic evaluation, Dr. Filipek confirmed that Mason was on the autism spectrum.

At this point I had done enough reading about autism that I felt a little more hopeful, and the diagnosis lit a fire in me. Now we knew: Mason was going to face challenges, and I needed to be there for him in a meaningful way. I quit my job with the consulting firm in part so I could start my own firm and work from home.

We learned that routine was critical for Mason's well-being. We went through flash cards every morning to make sure we did the right things in the right order. God help us if we strayed from the magic formula; any shift from the plan would upset Mason's apple cart.

I remember desperately trying to teach Mason about the idea of choice. Mason had echolalia, which is a common characteristic of communication with autism that involves verbal imitation. Something as simple as asking Mason "Do you want chocolate or vanilla ice cream?" would be met with the response, "chocolate or vanilla."

"No, chocolate *or* vanilla?" I would ask again.

"Chocolate or vanilla," he would repeat.

He wasn't registering that he could choose one or the other. I remember feeling so helpless as I stood in the kitchen with Mason, showing him the individual cartons with dramatic emphasis, yet totally lost as to how to get through to him.

Being involved at Mason's elementary school was important to me. I wanted to be a part of his school life so I could understand the people and dynamics that were, in part, shaping his school experience. The teachers, however, weren't really sure what to do with a male volunteer. I could tell they were a little uncomfortable handing me a stack of construction paper and a pair of scissors; but hey, those hearts and snowflakes weren't going to cut themselves!

My obvious lack of crafting skills led to launching a program at the school, called Watch Dog Dads, to help fathers be more involved in volunteering. We worked with the school to come up with father friendly volunteer roles, like helping out on the playground and teaching struggling kindergartners the magic motion that would pop open their milk cartons. (Seriously, without guidance those little fingers didn't stand a chance against the tiny milk cartons.)

By second grade, I started to notice Mason wasn't relying on his morning flash cards anymore. He still followed his routine with military precision, but he didn't need the cues. He was learning to self-regulate.

At Thanksgiving that year that we had a house full of guests. It was loud and chaotic, every room buzzing with activity. The kitchen was full of cooks, the living room was full of football talk, and for Mason, his home was full of overstimulation. I vividly remember Mason tugging on my sleeve, asking if he could have a time-out.

When Mason was out of control, we had a spot where he would sit and watch the time-out clock. When the time-out was up, he was free to move around again. This Thanksgiving, Mason wanted to go and sit quietly in the corner. He needed a break, and he knew it. What had previously been a punishment for Mason had transitioned into a respite, a place where it was OK for him to escape and recompose himself. This was a massive eye-opener for me. It also made me realize that Mason's "bad behavior" when he was younger could have been a product of overstimulation, not naughtiness. Time-outs were Mason's break from the barrage of stimuli.

In time, reading became Mason's regular intermission from the world. The boy with the pronounced speech delay plowed through *The Time Machine*, by H. G. Wells, when he was seven years old. From *Doctor Who* to Doc Brown in *Back to the Future*, Mason was transported to a land far away when his nose was buried in a book. This child who struggled with words couldn't get enough of them in printed form. Words leaped off the page; his comprehension was rich and meaningful. It was the ultimate irony, one that I believe only God could orchestrate.

Yes, Mason worked incredibly hard to speak fluently and boost his Lexile level. But I believe there's more to it.

Were you ever told that you could be anything you wanted to be? That if you put your mind to it, you could become whatever you dreamed? That with perseverance and grit, you could make it happen?

This is a very common line of encouragement parents take, with only the very best of intentions. But it's a false premise. In fact, it's a lie. Kids cannot be whatever they like.

In his book *Scatter*, my friend Andrew Scott states,

> Millions of dollars are spent annually by students and parents to pursue careers they were not made to live out, careers that don't fit and they will never grow into no matter how hard they try. ... We are not *called* to the purposes of God; we are *made* for them. God has designed us uniquely to be who He intends us to be and do what He intends us to do.[11]

In other words, you, me, and Mason ... we can't be whoever we want to be. But we can be exactly who God made us to be.

Chocolate or Vanilla

Mason will be finishing college soon. He is studying writing and rhetoric and would like to write as a career one day. God clearly made Mason to love language and words, in spite of his "disability." In fact, if you met him today you'd probably never even guess he's on the autism spectrum.

While Mason is my son, God made him to be very different from me. And because of Mason's passions and what he's been through in life, he has the unique ability to reach people with God's love whom I could never reach. He just needs to use what God gave him. He's been uniquely shaped—just like you and me—for a purpose.

When the time comes for Mason to move out, I'm not sure how I will feel when I see the boxes stacking up in the hallway. Will he carefully roll up his *Back to the Future* posters to mark a new era in his life? Which books will he choose to take? Will his origami inventions stay behind, or will they go too?

When Mason was born, my love for him was unlike anything I had experienced on earth. Over the past twenty-one years that love has transformed from one which shelters and protects to a kind of love that relaxes its grip and lets go. I am choosing to trust God as I release this remarkable, precious human being into the world.

Mason will always be my child and my biggest hero. I know he will fly. He was made for this.

17

Free to Love

Without courage, all other virtues lose their meaning.

—**Winston Churchill**

In the fall of 2015, I attended a worldwide conference for church and ministry leaders in Seoul, South Korea. I was intent on learning how the books, curriculum, and music tools available through my publishing company could serve the global church. But God had other ideas.

My friend, coworker, and travel partner, Kay, had some church connections in Seoul and had set up a lunch meeting for us the day before the conference began. Traveling with Kay is always an adventure, as he has friends in just about every corner of the world. When we arrived at the small, out-of-the-way restaurant, we were greeted by an older man and a younger woman, both Korean and both serving as part of a local church.

We enjoyed good conversation about families, children, and life in general. I was curious about the ministries of the church, and they were curious about what resources we might have in Korean.

Near the end of the meal, I commented that this was my first trip to Seoul and I was surprised at how close we were to the border with North Korea. I wondered how the separation between North and South impacted the daily life of their church members. After asking what I thought was a fairly logical question, the man and woman began to whisper to each other, nodding their heads. The woman finally turned to me and spoke.

"Actually, our brother here," motioning to the man, "is originally from the North, but has been here for a number of years now."

"Really? What? I have so many questions!" I said. "How did he get here? I'm guessing he didn't simply walk across the border. What was the journey like? And what impact does that have on his life here in the South?"

Over the next hour I listened intently as Chi (not his real name) shared his story. I'll relay it here, but I've changed a few key details to help protect his identity and prevent further repercussions for his family.

Chi's life in the North was difficult—always. Food and basic necessities were very difficult to come by, but you would never dare complain. The supreme leader of North Korea was God, and in theory he provided for everyone's needs. He was not viewed as a politician or even a king. He was revered as the creator of all things.

After an especially difficult few years, Chi began to think about escaping. He didn't have a wife or children, so he felt that leaving the North might be possible. He didn't have anyone to slow him down, so he would have a better chance than most.

Chi had also recently heard that there were families outside of the country who were still searching for evidence of where their loved ones had died during the Korean War. War paraphernalia was a premium and, under the right circumstances, a ticket to an audience. The right evidence or documentation could afford someone a secret communication line with outsiders. Luckily for him, Chi had come across a set of dog tags years ago and now realized they might be his gateway to freedom.

After communicating back and forth with a few contacts, Chi finally made a connection with a legitimate broker and heard there was indeed someone outside of North Korea who was interested in the dog tags. The broker was in fact a smuggler, willing to help Chi get across the border in exchange for a fee and the dog tags, which the smuggler could then sell to the interested party. They worked out a few details, and then set a day and time for the illicit border crossing.

On the evening of the escape, Chi made his way to a remote part of the border between North Korea and China. Crossing directly into South Korea was far too difficult and dangerous. So his journey to the South would take him thousands of miles circuitously through China, Laos, Vietnam, and Taiwan before he would eventually board a final ship bound north for South Korea.

Chi carried immense fear. There were too many moving parts. The smuggler wanted the dog tags; the guard wanted his payment to look the other way. The panic that consumed him was not about any one person in particular, but rather about how precarious the whole situation really was. What if the guard decided to take the money but also arrest him? What if the smuggler took the dog tags and then turned him over to the guard? What if other members of the North Korean army were on hand to witness his escape, but they were not part of the paid posse?

Chi's fear was palpable, overwhelming him with every step forward. He knew that if he was arrested, he would be put in a prison camp or killed. In North Korea, no grace was afforded to those who attempted to flee.

LOVE CHILD

Summoning every ounce of courage and strength that he had, and realizing this was the moment his life was going to change one way or another, Chi approached the border crossing. As planned, the guard turned from his post, leaving the fence line clear. After crossing the first barricade, Chi's heart leapt into his throat as he heard the voice of the guard call out to him. It wasn't an angry or impassioned shout, but more of a calm and quiet whisper. "Hey there, do you see that light in the distance?" the guard asked, pointing to a hilltop on the Chinese side of the border.

Chi looked to see a small lit sign with two crossing lines. "Yes," he replied.

The guard continued, "I don't know what that is, but I've heard people go there for help. If you get in trouble, go there."

As it turns out, the two crossing lines were actually a cross. After taking extreme caution to ensure he wasn't followed from the border, Chi slowly made his way toward the cross. Tired, hungry, and badly worn from the journey, he approached the door of the church.

Safely inside, this man who had bravely escaped perhaps the most oppressive regime on earth learned of Jesus and his love for the first time. For several months, Chi received discipleship, food, and medical care. Ultimately, he obviously had to continue the journey and make his way onward to South Korea. The trip would take several months, but the church provided him with a plan, contacts in South Korea, and finances to help him make the trek that would span thousands of miles. Chi set off as a brand-new man.

"But why was it so important to go to South Korea?" I asked. "Why not just stay in China? Or in any other country along the way?"

"I knew that in South Korea I would have a better chance of finding someone who could tell me about my family in the North. I wanted to hear how they were doing, because I knew that once it was discovered I had escaped, my family would be punished for my actions. You see, in North Korea the authorities pay villagers to inform on each other. You can win a good reward for identifying the family of someone who escaped. I wanted to go to the South so that I could hear how my family was doing."

"And how are they?" I asked.

Chi's face dropped and his demeanor changed. Years of weather and wear were instantly apparent as the weight of his family's well-being bore down on his shoulders. He had initially thought things might not be so bad because his brother held a high position in the government. But after a number of inquiries back and forth, Chi learned that his father, once a prominent dentist, had been sent to a prison camp in the far north of the country. Chi's brother had also been removed from his honored post and given the duties of a farmer. And Chi's nieces, were now barred from attending school. Three generations were punished for Chi's actions.

"I'm so incredibly sorry," I said. "I can't imagine how that must make you feel. There really are no words."

At this point, Chi stopped talking. I think he was out of words as well.

The young woman filled the painfully vacant air. "For the past several years, Chi has been using many methods and ways to share the gospel and truth of Christ's love with his friends and family in the North," she said.

She elaborated, reminding us that Chi never knew who heard the message or what might come of it. But he always hoped and prayed that his family members would receive the good news and that, perhaps through him, learn of the amazing way that God—not the supreme leader, but the real and true God—loves them without bounds.

"There is nothing in North Korea that comes close to the love of Jesus," Chi said. "This depth of love, hope, and desire for the future doesn't exist in the North. Therefore, I have no better way to spend the rest of the life God has given me than by doing everything I can to love those who, like me, never imagined something could be so wonderful."

God is relentlessly in pursuit of our hearts, drawing souls to him in part through the faith, love, and persistence of his disciples all over the world. Even when things look bleak, God is able to work, often in miraculous ways.

The book *Aggie: The Inspiring Story of a Girl Without a Country*,[12] relays God's goodness through the heartache of a young missionary couple. In 1921, David and Svea Flood left their home in Sweden for the Belgian Congo in Africa. The couple felt called to take the gospel to a remote village, so they went to N'dolera with their two-year-old son and another Scandinavian missionary couple, the Ericksons.

Upon arriving at the village, they were spurned by the chief. He didn't want the missionaries there for fear of alienating the local gods. Undeterred, the Floods and Ericksons walked up the slope, beyond the village borders, to set up camp.

They prayed for God to create a way for them to connect with the villagers, but aside from a young boy who was allowed to sell them chickens and eggs twice a week, they were shut out from the community. Svea Flood decided that if the young boy was the only African she could introduce to Jesus, he would be her focus. So she talked with him whenever he would come by, in the hopes of leading the child to Christ.

Malaria was a constant and imminent threat to the group, striking the Floods and Ericksons with such voracity that the Ericksons decided to leave the village and return to the central mission station in Africa. The Floods chose to stay, committed to the village of N'dolera.

Svea and David were subsequently blessed with a pregnancy amid the native landscape. When Svea went into labor, the village chief showed her compassion, allowing a midwife to assist her with the baby's birth. Svea gave birth to a baby girl, whom they named Aina.

The delivery took a lot out of Svea, who, at only four feet, eight inches tall, was already weak from her bouts of malaria. Just seventeen days after giving birth to Aina, Svea died.

David Flood was wracked with grief over the death of his wife, and he snapped. After burying his twenty-seven-year-old wife in a makeshift grave, David took his son and baby daughter down the mountain, back to the central mission station. Not knowing how to care for a newborn alone, he handed Aina to Mrs. Erickson and told the couple that he and his son would be headed back to Sweden. "I've lost my wife, and I obviously can't take care of this baby," he said. "God has ruined my life."

David headed for the port, turning his back on his missionary post, on Africa, and on God himself.

Less than a year later, the Ericksons died within days of each other from a mysterious illness. Baby Aina was handed over to American missionaries, who changed her Swedish name to Aggie; and when the little girl was three, they took her to the United States.

The couple loved little Aggie and were afraid to return to Africa with her in the event that some legal detail or paperwork hurdle would compromise their custody of the little girl. Instead of risking separation from this sweet orphan child, they stayed in their home state of South Dakota, working in pastoral ministry and raising Aggie as their own.

Aggie eventually graduated from high school and attended North Central Bible College in Minneapolis, where she met, and married, Dewey Hurst. Together, the Hursts built a prolific ministry. They had a daughter and a son, and in time Dewey was hired as president of a Christian college in a suburb of Seattle, where there was a prominent Scandinavian influence.

One day Aggie received a Swedish religious magazine in her mailbox. She didn't know where it had come from, and she couldn't read the words, but within its pages she found a black-and-white photo of a grave with a white cross, bearing the name SVEA FLOOD.

Aggie immediately sought the help of a college faculty member who could translate the article. The instructor offered a high-level summary, saying it was about missionaries who had served in N'dolera and given birth to a white baby. The young mother died, and one little African boy had been led to Christ. When the boy had grown up and the whites were gone, he persuaded the village chief to let him build a school. Eventually this young African man won all the students, and their parents, to Christ. The chief also eventually became a Christian. Now there were six hundred believers in N'dolera.

Aggie was floored over the fruits of her parents' sacrifice.

In recognition of the Hursts' twenty-fifth wedding anniversary, Dewey's college presented the couple with a vacation to Sweden. While there, Aggie intended to find her real father.

David Flood had remarried, fathered four more children, and become an alcoholic. He had also recently suffered a stroke. According to his children, David's bitterness toward God had not diminished with time; his family could clearly state David's one rule: "Never mention the name of God, because God took everything from me."

Once in Sweden, Aggie met her half-brothers and half-sister in person for the first time. She relayed her wish to see their father, but the siblings hesitated. They said she could try talking with him, even though he was very ill, but that she should not mention the name of God, because it would cause him to become enraged.

Not to be discouraged, Aggie went ahead with the meeting. She entered her father's filthy apartment with liquor bottles strewn everywhere and approached the aged man lying in an untidy bed.

"Papa?" she said gently.

He turned his face to the wall and began to weep. "Aina," he said, "I never meant to give you away."

"It's all right, Papa," she replied, embracing him gently. "God took care of me."

Her father's back became rigid, and his tears stopped flowing.

"God forgot all of us. Our lives have been like this because of him." He turned his face back to the wall.

Aggie gently touched his face. "Papa, I've got a little story to tell you, and it's a true one. You didn't go to Africa in vain. Mama didn't die in vain. The little boy you and Mama won to the Lord grew up to win that whole village to Jesus Christ. The one seed you planted just kept growing and growing. Today there are six hundred African people serving the Lord because you were faithful to the call of God in your life. ... Papa, Jesus loves you. He has never hated you."

The old man's body relaxed as he gazed directly into his daughter's eyes. He began to talk, and by the end of the afternoon he was fully restored with the God he had resented for so long.

Aggie and her father enjoyed their time together while the Hursts were in Sweden. Just a few weeks after the couple returned to America, David Flood passed away.

Years later, the Hursts were attending an evangelism conference in London where the superintendent of the national church in Zaire (formerly the Belgian Congo), representing approximately 110,000 baptized believers, delivered a report on the spread of the gospel in his nation. After his presentation, Aggie approached him to ask if he had ever heard of David and Svea Flood.

"Yes, madam," the man replied. "It was Svea Flood who led me to Jesus Christ. I was the boy who brought food to your parents before you were born. In fact, to this day your mother's grave and her memory are honored by all of us."

The two embraced in a long, emotional hug. Then he continued, "You must come to Africa to see, because your mother is the most famous person in our history."

In time, Aggie and her husband made the trip to Zaire and were welcomed by cheering crowds of villagers. Aggie even met the man whom her father had hired to carry her down the mountain in a hammock-cradle when she was an infant.

After the greetings were over, the superintendent brought Aggie to her mother's simple white cross. There

Free to Love

she knelt in the soil to pray and give thanks for her mother's servant spirit and ultimate sacrifice. Afterward, back at the church, the superintendent read from John 12:24: "Very truly I tell you the truth, unless a kernel of wheat falls to the ground and dies, it remains only a single seed. But if it dies, it produces many seeds."

Friends, God plays the long game. If we can put aside our fears, we have the privilege of stepping into his mission and playing our part in eternity.

18

Going Septic

A ship is safe in harbor, but that's not what ships are for.
— William G. T. Shedd

I think a fear of unsafe situations is drummed into us from the time we are very young. "Look both ways before you cross the street!" "Don't touch the hot stove!" Or in my case: "Don't jump off the second-story roof! That large trash bag won't work like a parachute!"

My poor mother had her hands full.

We're taught specific instructions for what to do in various emergency situations, like fires—and growing up in California, like earthquakes. My personal favorite was that in the event of an earthquake at school you should "crawl under your desk and put your butt toward the window." The logic was that it's better to pull shattered glass out of your butt than out of your face, but as a six-year-old learning this rule, it was just funny to hear adults talking about butts.

In our homes, in our cars, and in public spaces, safety is consistently a high priority. We avoid "bad" neighborhoods at night. We buckle our kids in age-appropriate car seats; and when they're learning to walk, we put soft, protective guards on any and all sharp corners, such as coffee tables and fireplace hearths.

LOVE CHILD

We're inclined to go especially crazy with safety measures in regard to kids. Today's helicopter parents fly well beyond the airspace of their children's academic lives, ensuring that their kids are safe in all physical, digital, mental, and emotional realms.

As a parent myself, I understand the inclination. It's our job to protect our children and to teach them to say no to things that feel unsafe. But for us adults, let's raise our viewpoint a few thousand feet and reflect on this question: Where does our desire for personal safety intersect with God's desire for us to step out and trust him?

Centuries ago, amid epidemics that ravaged the Roman Empire and made people very afraid, Christians bravely stepped out and brought hope to others. Sociologist and historian Rodney Stark described Christian witness at that time:

> Alien to paganism was the notion that because God loves humanity, Christians cannot please God unless they love one another. Indeed, as God demonstrates His love through sacrifice, humans must demonstrate their love through sacrifice on behalf of one another. Moreover, such responsibilities were to be extended beyond the bonds of family and tribe, indeed to "all those who in every place call on the name of our Lord Jesus Christ." These were revolutionary ideas.[13]

Yet this historical, documented show of strength and faith and trust in God has not carried through on a mass scale over time. In countries all around the world, safety has been a clearly stated reason for why Christians have avoided taking risks for the gospel. In fact, the research revealed that the fear of getting hurt or allowing our loved ones to get hurt was a primary reason Christians

Going Septic

put off living a life fully guided by God's mission. Fear tells us to take care of ourselves before thinking of others—to stay safe and stay home.

The amygdala is the region of the brain most commonly associated with our fear response. This makes it primal—i.e., something that rises up within us, a biochemical reaction that is most closely aligned with our "flight or fight" response and which is designed to optimize our chances for survival. When you face an angry grizzly bear, or you are approached by someone in a dark alley, this is the mechanism that kicks in. It's tough to control, because it's what our body does on autopilot. We either battle to the death or run like we've never run before. The response is beyond our consciousness; it's flying through our veins.

However, there is also an emotional component to the way we react to fear. Fear, or thinking about fear-inducing scenarios, can trigger the release of the same chemicals as those released due to happiness or excitement, and this makes our response personal. Do we perceive it as positive or negative? Exciting or scary? Thrilling or dangerous? Our reactions are very individualized.

Fear, of course, also represents a loss of control. How do we personally view situations that threaten our perception of control? Are we willing to release our grip on what we think we can control? Or do we want to grab on tighter and resist? Well, it's up to our own emotional lens.

Or is it?

I believe that we, as Christians, should be choosing every day to look at our fears through God's eyes rather than through our own. What is my perception of uprooting my family and moving to another country to work?

LOVE CHILD

> Hmm … There are so many unknowns! Where will we live? How much money will I be paid? How will my kids do in a foreign school?

Now let's compare that reaction to what I believe is *God's* perception of me uprooting my family and moving to another country to work.

> Excellent! I can't wait for you to meet my children in another land, and for you to introduce me to those who don't know me yet. This experience will grow you, expand your horizons, and allow you to experience new places and people in my creation.

God calls us to step out and trust him. We are to seek safety in *him*—not in the police, or our government, or the stock market.

If you're like me, where I place my trust actually shifts depending upon the situation and context. But more often than not, I've discovered that the more I can let go of human sources of safety, the more space there is for me to trust God with the results. And if I can truly trust God with the results *and* with the safety of myself and my family, then I should stop worrying about what people think of me, what my neighbors will say, and a host of other fears that stop me from embracing what God has so clearly commanded me to do on his behalf.

I have the pleasure of working alongside a number of people with truly inspirational and miraculous stories of how God has intervened to guard their personal safety while they were in the midst of doing his work. One of the most incredible stories involves a man I'll call Ezra.

Many years ago, Ezra left the comfort of his Western European home to go live in a remote village in the Middle East. Ezra went simply to live among these Muslim people

Going Septic

as a Christian and to share Christ's love through his life and actions. The home he lived in happened to be next door to a woman who was well known as the village prostitute. One day, during a casual conversation with this woman, Ezra learned that her septic system was clogged and had stopped working. She had called others to come look at the problem and fix it; but because of who she was, the men of the village would never dare to be seen at her home during the day.

Without hesitation, Ezra went next door, stripped down to his undershorts, and climbed into his neighbor's septic tank. After a short while, he found the problem and fixed her septic system.

While Ezra was waist-deep in his neighbor's sewage, a small group of men from the village knocked on Ezra's door. They had been watching him for quite some time, knew he was a Christian, and had come to drag him into the street and kill him. Since Ezra wasn't home to answer the door, the men decided to come back again the next day.

After the woman's septic tank was fixed, word quickly spread in the village about what this foreigner had done to help his neighbor in need.

The next morning, there was a knock at Ezra's door and he went to answer. Outside the door he found one man from the village. The man said, "We know that you don't believe what we believe, so yesterday some of us came here to kill you, but you weren't home."

He continued, "When we came here to kill you, you were next door wading in your neighbor's filth to fix her problem. I've come here alone this time because I want to understand what you believe. I want to know what would motivate someone to do what you did for your neighbor."

LOVE CHILD

Ezra invited the man in, and they talked for a short while. The man came back again the following day, and they continued the conversation. Ezra shared about how Christ loves us and talked about his own stories of faith. The man was overwhelmed. As a result of that conversation, the man invited Ezra to meet the other men who had planned to kill him and to share with them what he believes.

Some of the men have since become Christians. But even those who aren't yet believers continue to invite Ezra back for more discussions. And they even invite him to social gatherings with larger groups, so that he can share what he believes.

Ezra had many fears about safety before moving to that village. But he that knew this life was not his. It was God's. That's not just a Sunday school line; Ezra's faith in God was and is bigger than his fear in regard to his own well-being.

To put it another way, Ezra knew that there are only two possible answers to God's call. It's a yes-or-no question. If our answer includes the words "Yes, if …" or "Yes, but …," then our answer is really no. It should never be a question of "if," but rather a question of "how."

Whenever I meet people like Ezra, I always like to think of their roots. Do you do that? When you hear of heroic people who have made an incredible impact in the world, do you think about where they came from? Have you ever wondered what Mother Teresa was like as a teenager? Or if six-year-old Martin Luther King Jr. was a leader on the playground? Did twelve-year-old Dietrich Bonhoeffer stand up to bullies in the neighborhood?

Everyone has a history, and every person's backstory contributes to who they ultimately become. Some young people are wise beyond their years, with strong moral characters that mature further with age. Other kids, like me, end up doing a 180, building adult lives that are nothing like their childhoods. Yet, positive or negative, all of us carry threads from our formative years that can be found in the fabric of our adult lives. It's part of our life story, and God can use it in time for his glory.

I've had the honor of serving alongside hundreds—even thousands—of people who have actively and bravely given their entire lives for God's work. Not a single one of them has ended up even close to where they began. And I don't just mean geographically. For each person, investing wholly in God's mission has produced a personal transformation in the spiritual, physical, and emotional realms.

In 2019, I found myself sitting at a conference table in India across from three amazing women. All three of these women came from the lowest level of the lowest class in India's caste system. They had all been born into temple prostitution, just like their mothers before them. As temple prostitutes, also known as *devadasi*, their bodies were not their own. They were each married off to the temple god in an elaborate ceremony at a very young age, and then their virginity was sold to the highest bidder once they reached puberty. After that, they became sex workers in order to make money for their families. These young ladies experienced horrifying brutality that yielded unimaginable trauma.

A local Christian physician encountered these three women and began counseling and mentoring them. She encouraged them to start seeing themselves as God sees them—as incredible, precious, and wholly loved children. Over the course of time, these courageous women, with the doctor's help, realized that they had dignity and worth that extended beyond what society and culture dictated. The class of their mothers would not determine their value.

The devadasi practice actually became illegal in India in 1988, but because it has such ancient roots it has persisted in the shadows. So these women started fighting for the rights of devadasi, working to bring this system of sex slavery into the light. Their hope is to heal generations of women just like themselves.

Their operative word became *no*. *No*, they would no longer be used by men. *No*, they would not be assaulted and raped without recourse. *No*, they would not accept this brutal tradition. They held firm, even in the face of extreme violence and retribution. Threats and admonition would not quiet them. They were on a mission.

At the time I met them, none of these women were Christians. "But they also don't believe in the lies of their false god anymore either," the doctor told me.

When you've believed for so long that the god of your city or area sees you as a worthless piece of trash, I can only imagine how long the road might be before you're willing to consider that a loving and caring God has been waiting for you.

While you may not know people who have been maliciously abused like these three women, there likely are people in your circles of influence who need to know the love of Christ. They need it like food and water. They are in their own place of bondage or injustice or pain or suffering. They need to see an example of the type of love that doesn't run away, abandon ship, or cut ties at the first argument or conflict. They need to experience a love that is moral, empowering, and honoring—a love that is reliable, trustworthy, and true.

Going Septic

As Christians, this is where we can really step up and make an impact, because we are fully equipped to show people God's love. I don't mean that we need to open our Bibles and show them passages or recite verses. Anyone can read Scripture. It takes a real Christ-lover to be there—I mean, to *really* be there. To show up when they don't expect it. To meet a need when it's needed the most. To surprise with a level of love that exceeds the norm. To pay a bill. To provide shelter. To offer connections. To be a mentor. To take in a child. These are the best ways to demonstrate Christ's love.

Deep, deep, deep, in our own wayward and broken hearts, we need to step into the identity that was given to us by our loving Father and feel what it's like to love someone no matter the cost. I believe we need this like we need air. And I believe we will be incomplete until we take those first steps and unexpectedly, relentlessly, and unashamedly love someone who doesn't expect it.

And who knows?—Maybe for you the baby steps begin at home, or in your extended family, or in your neighborhood. I encourage you to exercise those muscles, to really build them up. When you are strong in Christ's love, I think you'll find it to be second nature to seek out those who don't know God's love, and you'll be equipped to share it naturally. But to get there, we all need to push beyond our fears and trust God to meet us.

The funny thing is that when we expose ourselves to fear over and over again, our reaction to it adjusts. For instance, the way you get over a fear of public speaking is to force yourself to do it. Repeatedly. And each time you speak in front of a group, your brain starts to build up a feeling of familiarity, and it becomes a little less scary the next time. The same is true with other situations that may induce fear—e.g., initiating conversations with people you don't know, traveling to new places, changing your routine, taking a risk. The more you exercise new muscles, the stronger and more resilient you become.

Do you want to accept the chains that keep you moored to shore? Or are you willing to cut the ties that bind and explore the open water?

19

Get Up and Go

Until we care more about what God thinks than what other people think, we are never truly free.

—**Christine Caine**

In my mind, *should* is often a dirty word. There always seems to be more attached to it than the surrounding words. Sometimes it's laced with a heavy dose of guilt or judgment, sometimes it infects us with feelings of stupidity or shame. *Should* can make us feel like we aren't doing enough, so we must be pushed, coerced, and even guilted into taking action and doing more. I think the way we recoil to the word *should* is often reflexive—an internal chemical response to an outward social expectation.

"You should visit your grandmother in the nursing home more often." "You should stop making bad financial decisions." "You should go to the gym." The *shoulds* can cut like a knife when they come from others, and they can also create a heavy burden when they originate from our very own inner voices.

And yet when they affirm something that we know deep down is true, the shoulds can be just the kick in the pants we need. To turn them into something productive, we need to push aside the indignation and stubbornness and chagrin they cause, and instead focus on the core message. What do I need to do differently or start doing now or stop doing to address the issue at hand?

Every single day we have choices.

As Christians, we should choose to live for Christ. We *should*.

In his podcast, "Ask N. T. Wright Anything," theologian and Anglican bishop N. T. Wright said,

> The God who made the world made it in such a way that some of the most important things he wants to do would happen through humans in his image ... reflecting his love in the world. That's how he wants to work in the world. He doesn't want to come top down into the world. He wants to solicit our partnership. ...
>
> God has not made us as machines. He's not the celestial mechanic. God is a God who delights in giving freedom to his creatures, which is a huge risk. He takes the consequences of that risk in Jesus.[14]

I think this is beautiful because it explains God's intent in this world. He wants us to choose him, to live in relationship with him, to follow his lead, to respond to his commands, to partner with him in the grand mission of drawing others into the kingdom. Should we do it? Yes, we should. Out of guilt or shame or coercion? No. We should do it because that's what we signed up for when we became Christians. It was our original choice, and now it's our choice once again. And missing this ultimate opt-in means we're not experiencing the beauty and satisfaction of a trusting, loving, committed relationship with our Creator.

We are only Jesus followers if we go where he would go. I'm not saying this means you need to book a ticket

Get Up and Go

to Galilee. But Jesus was on a mission to introduce every person he met to his Father. He went to places others wouldn't go to, talked to people others would avoid, spent time with those perceived by others as not worthy, and stood up to really powerful people on behalf of those whom society had mistreated for years.

As Christians, we all signed up to be part of this movement. It's not about living a good life, loving your family well, pursuing truth and honesty, and in general, being a kind person. You can do all those things without God. Wrapping your whole life around his mission can't be achieved by half measures. We need to go all the way. This may sound overwhelming, but it's not. It's actually an exciting opportunity.

Every single day of our lives we can wake up and make the choice to live that day on purpose—in pursuit of a life in alignment with God's plan. We won't be perfect. No one is. But we can commit to do our best, twenty-four hours at a time.

Later on in that same podcast, a listener asked how God can give us full freedom, yet still be in control. N. T. Wright responded by saying,

> Is the conductor of the orchestra in charge? Yes, but the players all have freedom. The conductor's job is to give them the space to freely play the music they want to play. ... When someone sets up a jazz number, does that mean the players are less free because someone has told them what the harmonies are? No! They are more free, within the framework. They can now express themselves in ways that delight and surprise the friends who are playing with them. That's more like what's going on with creation.

LOVE CHILD

As Christians, free will has always been part of God's plan. I remember one seminary professor I had who was a master at bringing up new perspectives on stories we had all heard a hundred times. During one class he had us reflect on Genesis 1:4:

> God saw that the light was good, and he separated the light from the darkness.

He read the verse out loud, paused for dramatic effect, and then asked us, "Is God all-powerful?" Yes. "Can he do anything he wants?" Sure. "So why didn't he banish the darkness? Why cause both light and darkness to exist?"

After a ton of discussion, which likely involved a whole lot of incorrect assumptions, the best answer seemed to be that it was a setup for free will. That from the very beginning of time, before he had created humans, God knew he wanted us to have the choice to turn toward light or darkness, to follow him or not. Even before he made us, he knew that he wanted us to choose to love him and follow him. It has always been a choice.

So how are you going to express your faith to others? I think many people who grew up in the church in America may have a misconception that to be an effective, Great-Commission-focused Christian, you need to pound the pavement to talk about your faith. While I'm sure some people found their way to Jesus through an interaction like this, I think for the most part people are more receptive to a more natural, organic, relational approach.

Louie Giglio said it well, "When you are being transformed by the power of the word of God, you don't have to walk into the world and tell people what they ought to do. Instead, you can walk into the world and let people watch what the power of the word of God is doing in you." I love this because it gives us the freedom to use our transformed life as a way to open the conversation with others. It puts the emphasis on *living* in a radically different way and then talking about it when the moment is right, as opposed to talking first. You don't need to get weird, or approach people with an underlying strategy or scheme.

I once read that observing the life of a believer is one of the most influential factors in bringing someone to faith in Christ. That's a pretty compelling reason to spend more time focusing on how we live as an example of Christ's love, wherever we are. (Imagine that! Most people don't come to faith in Christ by getting proved wrong about their own beliefs or losing an argument. Keep that in mind the next time you're invited to hold a picket sign.)

If we look back at the early church in the book of Acts, the people who came to know Christ during that time frame had never heard of Jesus before. He was brand-new to them, and his followers were living lives that completely contrasted the lifestyle of the day.

Contrast that with today. In the US, Europe, and other parts of the world where the church has had a presence, many people *have* heard of Jesus and have also seen his followers in action. Or perhaps it's more accurate to say that they have seen his followers' inaction! It isn't uncommon to hear non-Christians refer to Christians as liars and hypocrites. Why? Because Christians claim our lives are transformed by Jesus, yet often our lives don't reflect any difference at all. The chasm that lies between what we Christians say and what we do doesn't just prevent people from being attracted to Jesus—it repels them. Why would someone be willing to completely transform their life if the new life they are promised is not something they can witness in the lives of other believers? There is no proof in the pudding.

LOVE CHILD

It is heartbreaking to me that people are missing out on a relationship with Jesus because they are judging him based on what they see in us. We have to try to change this. Yes, we are human and we make mistakes. Yes, we will continue to trip up. But we have to do better, and try to live lives that allow others to see Christ through us.

I believe this starts by acting like the church in Acts. We need to live counterculturally, embracing all people in a positive, beautiful way. We need to love all of our neighbors. We need to push for social justice issues, for racial reconciliation, and for equality. We need to live out the Scriptures that says we are all one in the eyes of God. No one is greater or lesser.

Before the time of Jesus, the idea of standing up for the underdog wasn't a thing. The gods were powerful, supernatural deities who maintained order in the universe. The concept that God—the one and only God—would come and die the death of a slave was not only unheard of, but it was also a game changer. And it started with an act. This sacrificial act was the beginning of an entirely new world and a new covenant, one that is available to every single one of us.

Christ turned the tables on the balance of power. "Blessed are the meek, for they will inherit the earth" (Matt 5:5).

As his followers, we need to turn the power dynamic in this world through our everyday choices. We need to stop sending the message that Christians are all talk, that we are either liars or we don't believe what we're saying, and that our words are empty.

Now is the time for the world to be served by Christians who lead with actions rather than words ... with our hands, not just our mouths. We need to demonstrate a notably visible difference from common culture. We need to love and serve as Jesus would; and then, when people wonder why we behave differently, share that we live this way because we follow Christ.

Don't start with words. It's like putting the Jesus fish on the back of your car and then driving aggressively or flipping people off in traffic. It's hard to wear the label of Jesus follower openly if we're not going to live it to the extreme every single day. Lead with actions, and then we can follow with words and share our faith.

It's common to hear Christians say, in response to a tragedy or great need, "I will pray for them!" or "My family will pray about that!" Prayer is good, but I think if we actually took it upon ourselves to *act* in the face of tragedy, trial, and need, we'd have a church that is a whole lot more attractional. We have to remember our God-given mission:

> Therefore go and make disciples of all nations, baptizing them in the name of the Father and of the Son and of the Holy Spirit, and teaching them to obey everything I have commanded you. And surely I am with you always, to the very end of the age. (Matt 28:19–20)

What exactly does it mean to "go and make disciples of all nations" in the context of your life? Is God asking all Christians to leave their homes and move in one big missionary migration? Not at all. But he is asking you to fully wrap your life around him and to align your heart with his heart.

It is our job each day to choose Jesus, surrender our lives to him, and see those around us through his eyes. Pursuing outwardly focused, relationship-driven lives is attainable. Jesus is absolutely the best example of grace, forgiveness, justice, and hope in the world. We can only be whole through him.

Make an effort this week to show love to someone. Prioritize it. If the guy behind you in the checkout line is impatient, let him go ahead of you. If your child's classroom at school is experiencing a lot of behavior issues, surprise the teacher with a special coffee or something from the bakery. And if you walk past someone who is yelling and holding a picket sign, guard your heart against getting frustrated or angry. We are all children of God, and that means we are all equally worthy of his love.

Start small this week—but start. You'll see that one step becomes two, which becomes three and then four. Soon you'll be in a place you never imagined.

20

Oh My Soul, Korea

When I pray, coincidences happen. When I stop praying, the coincidences stop happening.
—**William Temple**

After meeting the man from North Korea, whom I introduced in chapter 17, I thought my emotions couldn't possibly be more tumultuous. I was shattered and weary, yet at the same time hopeful. I was sad for my friend's relatives and grateful for his safety. I was worried for his family's fate and happy for his current state. I experienced a torrid flurry of feelings in one big messy ball of emotion.

My trip to Seoul was changing my life. More than I could possibly know.

After saying goodbye to my new Korean friends, Kay and I headed over to the conference to get signed in and collect our name tags and various other conference materials. We were very early, so the team was still getting set up. I noticed one other conference attendee sitting on the steps, but otherwise we were the only ones there.

I think this is a good time to let you know that after the traumatic events of recent years—my divorce; another attempted relationship, which proved to be another wrong road; a layoff; moving homes; and a host of other unrest that comes with divorce—I had made my relational intentions incredibly clear to God. I made sure he knew that I was not interested in dating, not interested in relationships, and not planning to pursue anything until my son graduated from high school. My focus would be on whatever ministry God placed me in and raising my son. That's all, folks. My soul was done.

The idea of a personal relationship seemed like a mountain too large to climb, since it held the potential for more chaos, which would only serve to complicate my life and, in all likelihood, push me over the edge to some sort of unrecoverable emotional breaking point. I had experienced more than thirty years of so-called "core relationships," which never proved to be long-term or trusted or stable. Deep down I know I certainly craved that sort of foundation, but I was in no position to consider that it might be a possibility for me in my lifetime, let alone anytime soon.

While my thinking brain had made the clear-headed decision that a relationship would not be in the cards, my feeling brain would crack every now and again. In my more vulnerable, private moments, I recall praying something like, "OK, God, I would only be interested in a woman if she puts her relationship with you above herself and me."

I feel like at that point, somewhere in the heavens, God smiled.

As the conference got going later that evening, I met Ricardo. Ricardo had arranged to take about a dozen ministry leaders from throughout Latin America to this event in Seoul, and was serving as one of two translators for the group during the sessions. The young woman I had seen on the steps earlier that day was the other translator.

"Hi, my name is Geoff." I shook her hand and handed her my business card.

Yes, I'm that type of idiot.

Oh My Soul, Korea

"Hi, I'm Belén." She smiled in a way that acknowledged my awkwardness.

Throughout the next few days of the conference, Belén seemed to be around every corner. It's almost as if she was stalking me. She was clearly interested in knowing more about this amazing, handsome, and awkward man, and thus was actively pursuing me.

(Her version of the story is a little different, but I'm writing the story here, so let's go with my version.)

On the last night of the conference, Kay and I joined this group of Latinos for dinner at a nearby restaurant. It was a traditional Korean restaurant, with sliding paper walls providing privacy, pillows for us to sit on, and space under the table where our legs folded obligingly. Dinner started around six, and Kay and I were joined by Ricardo, Belén, and four other Latino ministry leaders.

Now if you've ever experienced a different culture, you may know that meals and social gatherings are perhaps the fastest way to see obvious differences in cultural norms and interactions. This dinner gave me a humorous front-row seat to the clash between our Korean-restaurant hosts and our mostly Latino dinner guests.

After the eight of us sat down, the restaurant staff pulled the paper curtains and removed the extra pillows to ensure that the room and accommodations were the perfect fit for the size of our group. Twenty minutes later, two more Latino pastors arrived, and the restaurant staff happily added two more pillows. Ten minutes after that, three more pastors arrived, at which point the staff asked us to move to a different room with a larger table to accommodate our group. We were now thirteen in total.

After a starter course and a bit of conversation, two more Latino pastors arrived, so the staff brought more pillows. At this point, it was becoming obvious that the Korean hosts were getting frustrated, unaware that in Latino cultures the time you are to meet for dinner is often considered just a suggestion, and since the meal and conversation will likely go on for hours, arriving late is no big deal.

Over the course of the next hour and a half we continued to add people until our group totaled twenty and we had been moved to yet another table, another paper-curtained room, and perhaps every spare pillow the restaurant staff could find.

Each time we changed rooms, and each time we added more pillows, I noticed that Belén and I maneuvered to sit next to each another. I honestly can't tell you everything we talked about that night. I know I learned that she was born and raised in Chile, and that she had been serving with Youth with a Mission, or YWAM, for fourteen years, training Latinos to share God's love in many countries around the world.

After dinner that night, I went back to my room and kept thinking about the conversation we had. By the next day, the last day of the conference, I knew that at the very least I wanted to find a way to stay in touch with her. I think that something about the obvious distance between us—Belén in Chile and me in the US—made it easier for me to take a step forward and try to get her contact information.

But how would I go about asking Belén for her contact information without risking yet another awkward interaction? My emotional safety walls were still nice and high, so I had to be creative. I found the table where Belén and the rest of her group were sitting and made my way over to thank them awkwardly and in horrible Spanish for the great time at dinner the previous evening. And then I went around the table and took a selfie with each person "as a way to remember our time together." I'm fairly certain that the only photo that wasn't blurry was the photo with Belén. And I had to find a way, of course, to get her a copy.

My plan was brilliant.

With an abundance of help from social media and technology, what started as a couple of typed messages back and forth quickly ballooned into two-, three-, and even four-hour phone calls every day. I was still traveling quite a bit at the time, as was she. Yet somehow we managed to find the time across various time zones to get to know each other a lot better. I was enjoying our talks about life, God, family, and missions. And I was still completely skeptical and unsure of what could possibly result from this long-distance relationship. All I knew was that the distance was initially comforting.

But that feeling didn't last.

After around two months of long nights, early mornings, and deep conversations over computer and phone, one morning Belén dropped a bomb on me.

"I've been thinking," she said. "I don't think you and I should spend so much time talking anymore."

Yup, somewhere deep in my heart and mind I had been waiting for this moment. Abandonment. I knew it well. My walls instantly went up.

She continued, "We spend so much time talking that I'm having problems getting up early in the morning, which means I don't have my quiet time with God. And I don't think I should be spending the time talking to you if I can't even talk to God during the day."

LOVE CHILD

What? Did I hear that right?

My brain immediately raced back to the prayer I had shared with God so many months ago. And here it was, smack in my face: a woman who valued her relationship with God more than any potential relationship with me.

"OK," I said. "I wonder if maybe you and I should spend more time talking to God together? Maybe prayer time? Reading our Bibles? Devotions? What do you think about that?"

She agreed, but no sooner had she agreed than I could feel my heart begin to panic. What had I done? I just took a step closer toward this person. ... Was that smart? I'm safer on my own. I can't take another heartbreak. And yet we clearly enjoyed talking with each other. We had a lot in common, and her priorities aligned perfectly with what I had told God was most important to me.

My brain was telling me that all the important stuff was lining up, with no conflict, and that everything seemed to be making sense. But my heart was telling me to stop, run, and escape before I got too far in and ended up getting hurt again. This ongoing battle between my brain and my heart continued for the next several months.

I knew my heart was damaged. It wasn't operating from a place of health. So I had to defer to my brain, because it knew. It knew this was a situation worthy of taking a risk. There was no good reason to run.

Over the next year, God arranged for Belén and I to grow in relationship, even meeting in person on a number of occasions. In reflection, I can see that his hand was on it all. How else could I explain it? What were the odds that she would be invited to fly to the US to meet with a particular ministry, while at the same time I already had meetings on my calendar to travel to the same city ... and even the same ministry? On other occasions, I seemed to have exactly the right number of airline miles to fly out and visit her in Chile.

Somewhere in heaven, God was smiling.

As for Belén, the more real our relationship became, the more she struggled with the idea of considering a future with a divorced man. And not just a divorced man, but a divorced man with a son! As my heart and mind battled it out, Belén was wrestling with God's rules versus his grace.

I will be forever thankful to the mentors and friends who helped her work and pray through her hesitancy to a place where God's grace and love prevailed. If things had gone the other direction, I have no idea where my heart would be today. And equally, I have no idea where Belén would be.

Finally, our relationship hit the point where I felt like it was time to ask the big question. I talked with Mason, we prayed, I talked with more family and friends, prayed somemore, and then hatched a plan.

I reached out to Jose, a friend of Belén's in Chile, and told him that I wanted to propose, but I needed to make sure she was going to be in town if I was going to fly all the way to Chile from the US to surprise her. Most weekends she was meeting with a church somewhere to talk about missions, so I couldn't risk it. I needed Jose's help to keep her home.

He and his wife agreed to help. His wife called Belén to ask if she would help plan a surprise party for Jose because he had been sad lately about a few things. Being a good friend, Belén agreed. She planned the date and location and helped with the details, of course not knowing she was planning her own proposal. Everyone was in on it except her. I love it when a plan comes together.

LOVE CHILD

On the big day, Belén and her friends gathered in a park in Santiago, Chile, to make sure Jose knew how much he was loved. Or at least that's what Belén thought. Earlier that day I had flown in, rented a car, and was now hiding in the bushes wearing a tuxedo and holding a bouquet of roses. "Mira, mama, mira!" or "Look at the crazy gringo in the bushes," came out of the mouths of more than one young child who walked by. Meanwhile, I was texting Belén photos of the snow from my front yard in Colorado, reporting how cold it was and telling her that I hoped she had fun at the picnic.

As the picnic for Jose started, Jose handed Belén an iPad and said, "Hey, your crazy American boyfriend sent me a video for you." Feeling very awkward that I would do such a thing during Jose's party, she went ahead and hit play.

"Hi, Belén," said Mason and I from the video screen. I went on to explain that Mason had just downloaded this new app on his phone and we wanted to show her how it worked. Mason picked up the phone and filmed me as I got out of the car and stood in the parking lot. Then, with the touch of a button, I beamed away like something straight out of *Star Trek*. Always the actor, Mason turned the camera back to himself to reveal a horrified look—wondering where his dad had gone. When Belén turned around after the video, she found me standing there in my tux, roses in one hand and a ring box in the other.

I knelt down and asked her to marry me, while at the same time her friends revealed a large sign they had made with the same question.

She said yes.

In the end, we both took a leap of faith, trusted in God, and chose to lean toward love. Slowly and steadily, God is healing years of pain and hurt through this relationship that he built. We give it all to him and continue to let his voice lead us every day … as long as we can quiet ourselves and the worldly noise around us so we can actually hear him.

Before Belén, I didn't think I was good at relationships. For decades, my childhood whispered all of my inadequacies in my ear. The script played louder in my head when my first marriage went down in flames. Even my professional resume reflected too many departures that were not of my own choosing. Subconsciously, I wore these experiences like armor. The plates stacked up one on top of the other, creating distance between myself and those around me. I allowed the plates to keep people a comfortable distance away, forming a shield of protection that minimized the odds I'd need to take on more plates. Yet over time, the weight on my shoulders became too much to bear.

But Belén changed that. I could unburden myself and drop the layers. I was willing to be vulnerable with her and let down my guard. Through Belén, I experienced Jesus in a new way. His perfect love cast out my fear.

I'm so grateful that I went to Seoul, Korea. If I had stayed home, I wouldn't have met my wife. It's amazing what can happen when you trust God and pray.

21

The Greatest Love Story of All Time

I may not be a smart man, but I know what love is.

—**Forrest Gump**

The Bible is a great example of a compelling narrative arc. The Creator creates. The creation abandons the Creator. The Creator loves so much that he relentlessly pursues his creation, sending an over-the-top gift to redeem the object of his affection. Slowly but surely all of creation realizes that their Creator—their one true love—was there, patiently waiting for them all along.

From cover-to-cover, the Bible has all the key ingredients of an epic story. There's love, pursuit, rejection, waiting, passion, and—ultimately—reconciliation.

Yet I think a lot of people have missed the mark on what the Bible is all about. They mistake this love letter for a user's manual. The subject of the Bible is not religion, or theology, or morality, or rules. It's about God's intention to be involved in our lives.

The book of Psalms encapsulates this love story beautifully. The authors of the various psalms immerse us in God's kingdom, relaying the full biblical storyline in poetic verse. It's a richly nuanced expression of the full gamut of the human experience. The wishes, praises, longings, and sorrows expressed in Psalms invite us to engage wholly and deeply with God, reflecting on his presence throughout all our days, in good times and in bad.

> The LORD is my shepherd; I shall not want. He makes me lie down in green pastures. He leads me beside still waters. He restores my soul. (Ps 23:1–3a ESV)

As humans, we have a built-in yearning to be loved and accepted. We want the permission—and the accompanying freedom—to take off our masks and be seen, without feelings of remorse or shame. We want to be part of a community, without limits or disclaimers. We want the "yes!" without the "but … " that often follows.

We have all that and more in Jesus. God is in active, relentless pursuit of our hearts. He loves us to the core of our beings. And as with any quality relationship, he wants us to love him back.

Some people have turned their backs on God because they have been hurt by the church. Some people have the wrong image of who Jesus is. Some people simply aren't interested in spiritual things. And some people have never been told about this grand love story. A friend of mine was traveling in Syria and shared his realization of just how special this story is to those who have not heard.

> As I sat in a tent, sipping tea with a group of nomadic Bedouin men and women in Syria, I took the opportunity to tell some stories, starting with Abraham and the sacrifice of Isaac—a story not completely unfamiliar to those who practice Islam. Then I went back to Adam and Eve and the fall, working up through the New Testament and John the Baptist, who speaks of the Lamb of God who takes away the sins of the world. The Gospels

followed, with the life, teachings, and miracles of Jesus—and his death.

As I spoke of Jesus' death, I looked up and could see tears rolling down a grandmother's face, and it suddenly dawned on me. She had no idea how the story ends. She didn't know what was next. The cross, the crown of thorns, the hours of darkness, the pain, the loss. ... She didn't realize hope was coming on the next page.

This love story is tender and sacrificial. Christ was willing to die to bring us close to himself. From chapter to chapter, he is hands out, palms up, inviting us into a deep, meaningful relationship. Anyone who tries to make coming to faith in Christ a speedy or neat-and-tidy transaction is cheapening the profound value of this sacred bond.

Historically, Christians and the church have sometimes engaged in quick conversion practices. In the early 1500s, the Spanish demanded that all Native Americans convert to Catholicism—or "We shall seize your possessions and harm you as much as we can as disobedient and resisting vassals."[15] Can you imagine how this pained Christ, the lover of our souls?

Some churches used to take to the skies, dropping tracts all over a city and subsequently declaring it "saved." Several years ago, a church near where I was living held a carnival as part of their summer kids' camp. On the last day of the camp, the kids wore their swimsuits for water-balloon fights and other fun. At some point, each kid made his or her way into a pool for the play time. The church declared each child baptized and sent a certificate home with them at the end of the day. Some parents were more than upset, and the local newspaper caught wind of the story and reported on the church's tactics.

LOVE CHILD

A friend of mine told me about a Baptist church he attended as a kid. The pastor would sometimes refuse to stop preaching until someone "got saved." The guys in the youth group sat at the back of the church, and when they couldn't take it any longer they would push a kid into the aisle so that he could get saved and they could all go home for dinner. It didn't matter that some of the kids who were easy to push—or who had the misfortune of sitting at the end of the pew—were saved multiple times. Everyone knew what was going on. It was a means to an end.

When we make conversion just about securing the "yes," we diminish everything Jesus has done for us. We also devalue our response to what he has done as something that is fleeting, when it's really just the beginning. Because just as he never stops pursuing us, God is never done with us.

But to truly engage in this love story, we need to be present.

About ten years ago, a good friend of mine took a trip to Ethiopia with some pastors from the US. They went together to see the work of the church there and to experience worship with other believers. As it turned out, the church "building" was actually a lean-to made of 4x4 timbers holding up a corrugated metal roof. After a wonderful afternoon service, the pastor of the church sat with them over some strong coffee and a basket of *injera*, which is a fermented sourdough flatbread. The guests asked the Ethiopian pastor many questions about his ministry; and in turn, he asked many questions about theirs. They shared stories and had a great time of fellowship together.

As the American pastors were preparing to leave, one of them, an older man from Texas, turned to the Ethiopian pastor and said, "Thank you for opening up your church to us today. Please know that as I go back to my congregation, we will be praying for you and your great work here."

The Ethiopian pastor smiled and said, "Thank you, I always appreciate prayers for the work God is doing through our ministry here. And please know, we will be praying for you as well."

The pastor from Texas smiled and turned toward the waiting bus. As he was getting ready to step in, he turned back and said to the Ethiopian brother, "Do you mind if I ask ... When you pray for us, what would be your prayer?"

The Ethiopian pastor looked at him and simply said, "Well, as you know, we are a very poor village. We don't have much, but we have God. In America, you have God as well, but you also have so many things to distract you from him."

The general idea has been noted by many others before me, but it bears repeating: "Noise is an instrument the devil knows how to play beautifully." I'm not necessarily saying that iPhones are a tool of the underworld, but when mobile devices and the internet and podcasts and streaming television and social networks eat up our free time, we have no quality time with our Creator. As the Ethiopian pastor knew, the constant buzz of life is a distraction.

To submit ourselves completely to the one and only God who adores us, we must be vulnerable. To get to a place where we can be completely vulnerable, we need to be reflective. And to be completely reflective we need some time when we can be quiet.

The concept of "quiet" makes a lot of people nervous and uncomfortable. Do you need to carve out thirty minutes from your busy day to sit in silent contemplation? Do you have to get up earlier? Go to bed later? Lock your kids in their bedrooms so you can have some uninterrupted time? (I'm kidding. Don't do that.)

There's no one right way to be quiet with God. Everyone has to figure out what works best for them. I think it's important to remember, however, that this is a love story, and love doesn't fit in a box or thrive in a time block in your iCal. For me, being fully present in the world is one way I can grow in relationship with God, by quietly observing, experiencing, and mindfully participating in his creation. When I take my earbuds out on the train, there's a better chance I will notice the guy sitting nearby who looks like he could use some encouragement. When I stop checking email on my phone, I can help the older lady at the airport figure out how to find a hotel when her flight is canceled. When I turn off the television, I can look into my wife's eyes while we talk about her day.

> The King will reply, "Truly I tell you, whatever you did for one of the least of these brothers and sisters of mine, you did for me." (Matt 25:40)

When we slow down and embrace lives of care and compassion and service, we are picking up the script and playing our role in God's love story. By loving others, we are loving our Heavenly Father.

22

A Father's Love

Start children off on the way they should go, and even when they are old they will not turn from it.

—Proverbs 22:6

This verse makes me feel very conflicted. I mean, I get it. It makes sense. But looking back at my childhood, I was not "started off" well. I think my mom did her best with me, using the tools she had. It must have been so frustrating and exhausting for her. I'm not proud of my behavior or the havoc I wreaked.

As an adult, I know my childhood anger and outbursts came from pain and sadness and fear. I was insecure, I felt rejected by my father and others, and I didn't have the constancy of a community or family to keep me rooted.

If you ever studied psychology in school, you probably remember Abraham Maslow's hierarchy of needs. It's basically a pyramid with tiers that identify stages of growth in developmental psychology. The goal, of course, is to get to the apex, which is where you experience your full potential. But every member of society starts at the bottom of the pyramid, where our basic needs—like food, shelter, and clothing—are met. The next layer up is personal security, safety, and resources, followed by a layer of love and belonging, which includes friendship, family, and a sense of connection.

LOVE CHILD

Of the five tiers in Maslow's hierarchy, the bottom three were incredibly unstable for me. And according to Maslow's original theory, one can't progress to the next level until the previous level has been satisfied. I guess that makes sense in my life. I didn't experience safety, security, and stable relationships. Those lessons weren't part of my upbringing. Instead, I was always trying to keep my walls up. I didn't feel protected, so I protected myself, acting up and fighting to create one massive smoke screen that obscured any view of my vulnerability.

Yet when I look at my life as an adult, I can so clearly see what my mom did right. By making sure the church was the one element of stability in my life, she gave me a huge gift. She planted the seeds of faith in my spirit, and then did her best to water them throughout my upbringing. She modeled what it meant to have faith no matter what—even when times were tough. And while I didn't catch on until my college years that Christianity was a whole lot more loving and personal than I had originally understood, I am so grateful to my mom for weaving God throughout the core of my soul. I'm in my forties now, and I hope she can see the truth in Proverbs 22:6. I have not turned from what she started.

Looking back, my mom's faith has always been stable, at least from the outside. Her passion for years, even in the midst of extreme chaos within our little family of two, was intercessory prayer—praying for other people and circumstances. Even when I was little, I can remember the long list of names that she'd pray for every morning. This list served as a bookmark for her Bible and prayer book.

When I was in my twenties, my mother took vows to join a holy order of nuns focused on, among other things, intercessory prayer. The ceremony was beautiful and weird. It was beautiful in that the Episcopal bishop who performed the rights and ceremony made it very special and memorable. It was weird because, even as an adult, the child in me squirmed when my mother took vows of chastity outside of marriage. In the Episcopal tradition, nuns and priests can marry. And yes, we should all have chastity outside of marriage. But it's still an odd thing to hear your mother declare publicly in church, with the backdrop of a congregation and friends and family. And yes, almost instantly I realized that my mother was a nun and my father was a priest, and there was likely a great joke in there somewhere.

A few years ago, Mom's order shifted to the Anglican Church and away from the Episcopal Church as a result of tensions around the view and support of homosexuality in the church. I struggle with those topics. Not because I feel one way or another about the doctrine, but because I can't help but see yet another way the devil is happy that we are focusing our attention on anything other than the Great Commission. Among the thousands of church teams and leaders I've worked with over the years, I've heard a million excuses why churches are *not* focusing on the mission Christ laid at our feet. It's all distraction that keeps us from serving, loving, and growing the kingdom.

Nevertheless, Mom is still a nun. Actually, she is the Mother Superior of the order, which gives me the opportunity to call her my "mother Mother Superior"! It's a good thing, too, because I was running out of nun jokes and nun-related Christmas gifts, like the "Nuns on the Run" wall calendar filled with nuns having fun. My favorite image is of two nuns holding hands while roller-skating, with the caption, "No separation of church and skate."

LOVE CHILD

Every day, God is at work through our personalities. I believe our task and challenge is to be present. When I had the chance to spend time with the Northumbria Community at my spiritual retreat, I asked why there were four times of prayer each day. Many versions of the Rule of Life prayer have the same morning, noon, evening, and bedtime rhythm. One of the brothers answered, "Because this way we know that prayer and focused time with God is the thing we do most each day." I think that's right, and it's a practice that Christians have been doing for a very, very long time.

Despite the inevitable pain, disappointment, and hurdles that come our way, our lives are all leading somewhere. At times, we can be rightly discouraged by our journey and wonder where God is in it. When I look back at my childhood, it's only now, in my forties, that I have those aha moments. What if I had grown up in a perfect household, with two normal parents, and a dog, and three square meals a day, and sheets that smelled like Downy, and the right brand of jeans, and the right group of friends? I have no idea where I'd be today. But I do know that the childhood I was given has made me a man who is deeply committed to loving and caring for his family, a man who is not so much concerned with material things, and a man who wakes up each day with a desire to walk with God. My childhood setbacks were a setup for my life today.

I know the idea of serving God with your whole life requires some mental wrestling. In fact, I think it's probably one of the biggest spiritual battles for most people. It's the fight that starts the moment we say yes to following Jesus. We've got to fight back against our inclinations to control our destinies, manage our outcomes, and plan our days. I can tell you from personal experience giving up control is the most freeing thing in the world.

A Father's Love

So many people today are discontent with their lives. They think it might be their job, or their weight, or their house, or their spouse that is holding them back, so they search for fixes to their symptoms. I have been down that road myself. But I believe that the source of a discontented heart is a lack of purpose and, more accurately, the fact that we are missing the boat on our true reason for being.

Francis Chan explains it this way:

> There's a reason God gave us his Holy Spirit. It's so we could be equipped to serve as his witnesses on earth. When the Holy Spirit enters into us, we really *want* to make disciples and have an impact on people. We were made for this!

This doesn't mean that we need to head out and become Bible-pushers on the street. It means we use our own unique personality and life history and skills and approach to make meaningful connections with those around us. By allowing others to see how we live, and how we love Jesus, we have the privilege of helping people develop a heart for God. Our openness can instigate their willingness to find out what he's all about.

I have found that when we shift our life focus from ourselves to God, it is life changing for others and life changing for ourselves, as well. And this shift has connected so many dots for me. Now I can see the many positives that have come out of my chaotic childhood. The cumulative effect of the pain, paired with the influence of key people in my life—like my mom and Travis—pushed me into Jesus' arms.

I recently heard a clergy from the Philippines say, "People who have suffered know how to smile." Sometimes it takes suffering to seek a higher level of solace.

LOVE CHILD

As I was deepening my dependence on God throughout my twenties and thirties, I still had a dad-sized void in my heart. I remember lying on the couch one day, reading Donald Miller's book, *A Million Miles in a Thousand Years*. I came to the part of the book in which Don discusses the idea of reconnecting with his father. The hole in my heart suddenly began to feel extra hollow.

I started to imagine the idea of reconnecting with my own father. What would that even look like? I knew he was a lot older than my mom, so was he even still alive? What if I missed my opportunity and there was no longer even a chance?

I put the book down and picked up my laptop. After a bit of searching, I found what I thought was his address and began writing him a letter. I had so many questions, but after several drafts I came to the conclusion that all of my questions would be best asked in person. So I started over and simply asked if he would be interested in meeting me. I nervously licked the envelope, pressing it shut with my vulnerability tucked inside. I figured the worst possible outcome would be no response, so I tried telling myself I didn't have much to lose.

To my surprise, a few weeks later I received a letter back from my father, with an invitation to visit him at his home. He also included his email address to make planning a bit easier.

A few months later I pulled into his driveway, preparing for what could very well be the most awkward meeting imaginable. I hoped God was hearing my silent prayers for help. As a bead of sweat rolled down my back, I knocked on the front door.

I was greeted by hobbits.

A Father's Love

My father and his wife, who answered the door, were both very, very small. *Where did my 6'2" frame come from?* I wondered. *My mother is about 5'5".* ... My ruminations were interrupted by the warm smiles beckoning me to come in. My father was in his eighties, and his wife was in her seventies.

We fumbled through the initial introductions. I remember saying, "Hi. I'm Geoff—your son!" In response, he said, "Well, I guess that makes me Dad!"

In the time that had lapsed between my father's invitation and our meeting, including during my flight, I had been scripting questions I wanted to ask. I even prioritized them in case things didn't go well and my father asked me to leave. I wanted to be sure I front-loaded the conversation with the most important questions. I really had no idea what to expect, but I knew this might be my one and only shot at finding answers to questions that had plagued me throughout my life.

After some brief pleasantries, I dove in, direct and to the point:

- Why did you choose not to be a part of my life?
- Were you ever curious about me?
- How do you remember the relationship between you and my mother?
- Do you have any hereditary issues or diseases I should be aware of?

My father answered every question. I learned about the pressure he felt, both from my mother's family and from his family. I learned about his previous marriage, divorce and pain. I learned that in that dusty Tucson motel room, he didn't really see a choice.

This meeting gave me the missing half of my birth story. And no, not all the details added up between the version my mom shared and what he recalled. But more than forty years had passed, and in reality the truth probably rests somewhere in the middle.

Most importantly, I received my father's deep and sincere apology for not being a part of my life. And somewhere between the tears and gasping to catch my breath, I offered my forgiveness.

Over the past several years, my relationship with my father has grown. I have learned of my half-siblings and one of them has learned of me. It's a process, and it's not perfect, and there is still a lot of pain. But now my teenage son, infant daughter and newborn son have a grandfather.

God is good.

My father's relationship with God is anchored by the rhythm of praying four times a day, in the very same style and practice I was drawn to in my own spiritual journey. He's been doing it daily for the last fifty-plus years. When I heard this, I couldn't help but smile. It seemed to be a "like father, like son" moment. It was my first one, so I savored it.

My father's wife quietly pulled me aside one day to share that my father had prayed for me by name every day of my life. As I look on it now, I see both my mother *and* my father praying for me daily throughout my life. Yet somehow these two godly people allowed shame, hurt, and years of damage to thwart any sort of healing or restoration. They were two broken people who gave birth to a son who, as it often turns out, would grow up broken as well.

But I've found that healing can come when we push past our fears and step out in faith. We can't control the

A Father's Love

outcome, of course. My father certainly could have chosen to ignore my letter—or worse, rebuke my attempt to meet him. But if I hadn't made the effort to extend an olive branch, I'm not sure we'd be where we are today.

Every child should have the love and acceptance of their earthly father. Of course, not all do. Whether you've experienced an absent or unloving parent, or an abusive spouse, or ceaseless bullying, or the death of a child, or any number of tragedies and traumas, I can assure you that God can gently fill the hole in your heart. The love, acceptance, understanding, or peace you hunger for can be satisfied by Jesus. I'm not saying you get amnesia and never, ever again will remember past hurts. But you will be able to put it all in its proper perspective. We can only be responsible for our own choices and decisions. Everything else we relinquish to God, trusting he will sort it all out.

Knowing I am loved by my earthly father has helped bring a sense of healing to my heart. Knowing I am loved by my Heavenly Father to the core of my being gives me an overwhelming sense of gratitude and a passion to pay this gift forward for someone else: to share the Lord's great healing, hope, and love with those who don't know it.

No matter where you are in your life, no matter what bruises and scars you may have from the past, remember the words of Miss Addie. As long as we're still on God's earth, it must be for his purpose. And his purpose—to the ends of the earth, for all his children—is love.

Afterword

Here comes the sun, and I say it's alright.
—**The Beatles**, "Here Comes the Sun"

As I drove down Woodmen Road, I looked west, across Pikes Peak. It was a bluebird day, and streaks of warm winter sun gleamed across my windshield. The snow-capped mountains sparkled in the distance as I flipped on the radio. The song that was playing was "Way Maker" by Sinach:

You are way maker, miracle worker, promise keeper
Light in the darkness, my God
That is who You are

I looked in the rearview mirror and said, "Hey, Amanda …"

Without warning, my chest tightened, my voice cracked, and tears started streaming down my face. I couldn't finish my sentence. I couldn't get out any more words. I began to sob. I could hear Belén in the backseat begin to quietly sob with me.

We were driving home from the hospital with our newborn daughter, Amanda, and as we slowly made our way through the streets of Colorado Springs, we were both completely overwhelmed by God's goodness.

It was Christmastime, and this brand-new baby of ours was clearly a gift from God. Just as the baby Jesus brought peace and joy and hope to the world, Amanda, which means "loved one," was bringing peace and joy and hope to our family.

There were so many years when I didn't know if I would ever know real love, ever trust, or even experience real joy again. There were times when I was desperate for

God to change my circumstances. There were times when I questioned his plan. And there were times when I knew I simply had to keep putting one foot in front of the other and trust him while I walked. As I consider the journey, it is easy to see my life with him shaped through mutual devotion, hard work, and our relentless pursuit of each other.

Now, looking in my rearview mirror, I could see the precious fruit born out of a long and painful pruning.

Amanda was born on December 20, which is on the winter solstice in the northern hemisphere, the longest and darkest night of the year.

My journey has been long, but it has taught me that darkness never lasts forever. The sun always rises again.

Acknowledgments

Writing a book with personal details is a bit like making a time capsule out of a glass box and putting it on display. God keeps moving, and life keeps changing.

Since toiling over this book, God has gifted Belén and I with a little boy, adding Sebastian to the family, alongside Mason and Amanda. The foundation of love God has built through them grows better each day, and I will forever be thankful to each of them for making life an incredible adventure. I love you all!

To my good friends Dave and Dita, who encouraged me to write this book and even helped me figure out how to put one foot in front of the other to make it happen, I am tremendously thankful.

To the countless friends mentioned in these pages, thank you for sharing your stories and experiences. I hope you see how God used them as a little part of my ongoing transformation.

And to my mother, father, and others who raised me, thank you. It was not the easiest journey. God never gave up on any of us, and he never will.

Notes

1. George Barna, and David Kinnaman. "Do You Really Know Why They're Avoiding Church?" Barna Group. Barna Group, 2014. https://www.barna.com/churchless/.

2. Gregory A. Smith, Alan Cooperman, Besheer Mohamed, and Elizabeth Podrebarac Sciupac. "In U.S., Decline of Christianity Continues at Rapid Pace." Pew Research Center's Religion & Public Life Project. Pew Research Center, June 9, 2020. https://www.pewforum.org/2019/10/17/in-u-s-decline-of-christianity-continues-at-rapid-pace/.

3. "Signs of Decline & Hope Among Key Metrics of Faith," Barna Group: State of the Church, March 4, 2020; https://www.barna.com/research/changing-state-of-the-church/.

4. Sarah A. Schnitker, Thomas J. Felke, Justin L. Barrett, and Robert A. Emmons, *Psychology of Religion and Spirituality* 6, no. 2 (May 2014): 83–93.

5. Canadian Red Cross, "Breaking the Poverty Disease Cycle," https://www.redcross.ca/crc/documents/What-We-Do/Emergencies-and-Disasters-WRLD/education-resources/lucky_ones_povdisease.pdf.

6. Gina Zurlo, "The World as 100 Christians," Gordon Conwell Theological Seminary website, https://www.gordonconwell.edu/blog/100christians.

7. Todd M. Johnson and Gina A. Zurlo, eds. "World Christian Database" (Ledien/Boston: Brill), www.worldchristiandatabase.org. And "Church Giving Statistics, 2019 Edition," Pushpay website, https://pushpay.com/blog/church-giving-statistics/.

8. Barna Group, *Translating the Great Commission: What Spreading the Gospel Means to U. S. Christians in the 21st Century*, 2018.

9. OM.org/INT.

10. Joel Houston, Benjamin Hastings, and Michael Fatkin, "So Will I (100 Billion X)," from the album "Wonder," Hillsong Music Publishing, 2017, https://hill¬song.com/lyrics/wonder-album/.

11. Andrew Scott, *Scatter: Go Therefore and Take Your Job with You* (Chicago: Moody Publishers, 2016).

12. Aggie Hurst and Doug Brendel, *Aggie: The Inspiring Story of a Girl Without a Country* (Access Publishing, 1986).

13. Rodney Stark, *The Rise of Christianity: How the Obscure, Marginal Jesus Movement Became the Dominant Religious Force in the Western World in a Few Centuries* (San Francisco: Harper, 1997).

14. N. T. Wright, "Ask N. T. Wright Anything" podcast.

15. https://en.wikipedia.org/wiki/Spanish_Requirement_of_1513.

About the Author

Geoff's passion is to inspire people to be a living witness of God's love in the world. He speaks regularly on the common fears and barriers that prevent Jesus followers from accepting their role—and actively participating—in God's mission of love and compassion. His heart beats to encourage people to step beyond the safety of their comfort zones and experience the joy and freedom that comes with servanthood.

Geoff has spent the lion's share of his professional life at the intersection of marketing and mobilization for God's mission. Years of research in multiple countries has afforded Geoff a unique window into the hearts of Christians. Geoff's ability to see beyond the surface and identify real motivators among Christian audiences has translated into years of practical experience helping ministries to increase kingdom impact by improving how they inspire and equip believers.

Geoff is also the author of *The Family Business: A Parable About Stepping into the Life You Were Made For*. Geoff and his wife, Belén, have three children.

visit us at missionbooks.org

Karmic Christianity: Finding Peace by Faith Alone

E. D. Burns explains why the antidote to fear is not power but rather peace—God's peace. If we're honest, we know that our best is never good enough. We are frequently powerlessness to change our circumstances. Burns shows why the solution is not working harder, being better, or just giving up. Readers learn why we don't need to be exhausted. Instead, we can rest in God's refuge, trusting that his love for us is perfect in Christ.

Great Commission Spirituality: Abiding in Christ, Serving in Obscurity

E. D. Burns encourages any layperson, church leader, or missionary burdened by their vocation and calling to rediscover the joy of serving in reliance on Christ. By emphasizing that Christ lives in and works through us, Burns reassures readers that true fruitfulness in ministry comes from abiding in Christ, who orchestrates our work by his Word and perfect timing. This resource offers a robust theological framework paired with practical applications.

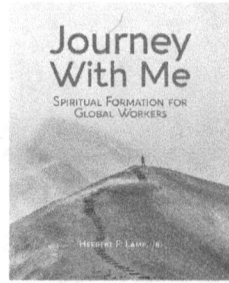

Journey With Me: Spiritual Formation for Global Workers

Herbert F. Lamp, Jr. invites us to prioritize soul care, rather than treating ministry as a replacement for intimacy by exploring over fifteen ancient spiritual graces—such as Lectio Divina, rule of life, silence and solitude, and prayer of Examen.. In the process of knowing and being known, God fills us up with his love, joy, peace, and wisdom. Only then can we minister to others, balancing a heart for God with hands for service.

www.ingramcontent.com/pod-product-compliance
Lightning Source LLC
Chambersburg PA
CBHW052139070526
44585CB00017B/1899